Mentoring
Early Childhood
Educators

Mentoring
Early Childhood
Educators

a handbook for supervisors,
administrators & teachers

Carol B. Hillman

Foreword by
Carolyn Caselton Spence

HEINEMANN
Portsmouth, NH

Heinemann

A division of Reed Elsevier Inc.

361 Hanover Street

Portsmouth, NH 03801–3912

www.heinemann.com

Offices and agents throughout the world

Library of Congress Cataloging-in-Publication Data

Hillman, Carol.

  Mentoring early childhood educators : a handbook for supervisors, administrators, and teachers / Carol B. Hillman ; foreword by Carolyn Caselton Spence.

    p. cm.

  Includes bibliographical references.

  ISBN 0-325-00883-3 (alk. paper)

  1. Early childhood teachers—Training of.   2. Early childhood teachers—In-service training.   3. Mentoring in education.   I. Title.

LB1775.6.H54 2005

372.1102—dc22   2005024198

Editor: Danny Miller

Production: Lynne Costa

Cover design: Joni Doherty

Typesetter: Valerie Levy/Drawing Board Studios

Manufacturing: Steve Bernier

Printed in the United States of America on acid-free paper

10 09 08 07 06 RRD 1 2 3 4 5

For Robert,

who is always there for me.

Contents

Foreword

An outstanding teacher of young children, a consummate teacher of teachers, a respected colleague and cherished friend—this is how I see Carol Hillman. I have known Carol for more than a decade. Our connection began when she worked as an early childhood consultant in the elementary school where I was the principal. As she visited classrooms, her sensitive spirit and knowledge of child development and best teaching practices shined brightly for all to see. Her keen observational skills were matched by her ability to listen intently and to guide with respect. She shared her insights and depth of experience, but most of all she posed thought-provoking questions. Her queries often prompted a teacher to redesign the classroom environment, to examine an instructional issue from another perspective, or to view a child in a new light.

During my work as a principal, I hired many new teachers. Each time, the same haunting thought pulsated through my mind: This person will influence the lives of hundreds of young children. Are this teacher's intellect and heart well prepared for this daunting challenge and awesome responsibility? Once one recognizes the power of a teacher to positively influence or irreparably harm a child, it becomes abundantly clear that the supervisors and mentors of teachers-in-training need to be our best educators. It is for this reason that I am thrilled and grateful that Carol Hillman has written *Mentoring Early Childhood Educators: A Handbook for Supervisors, Administrators, and Teachers.*

In this book, Carol continues to live her passionate commitment to children and to the field of early childhood education. Her writing is grounded in her profound beliefs about what young children need. These beliefs are supported by her years as a nursery school teacher and her experiences as a skilled supervisor of student teachers. Within the pages of this book, early childhood supervisors will discover, or be reaffirmed by, the importance of quiet observation, focused listening, trust building, clear, honest communication, and a commitment to positive, supportive relationships.

Mentors and supervisors of teachers-in-training need to instill in their students the ability to reflect upon every aspect of their teaching practice in order to grow and to be worthy of children. Since reflection is the key to lifelong professional development, I encourage each early childhood educator reading this book to do so with a commitment to self-discovery and professional renewal. With each chapter, I invite you to savor the guidance provided and the questions posed, and to be open to reexamining your own practices in the light of the model presented. Your teachers will benefit and, in turn, so will our children. The quality of what you give to your student teachers or teachers-in-training will reverberate in their classrooms for years to come.

I once asked Carol about feedback she had received from a group of student teachers with whom she had just finished working. One young teacher's words speak to the power and significance of an effective educational supervisor: "You inspired me to open my eyes wide and learn from all around me, especially from the children."

—*Carolyn Caselton Spence*

Carolyn Caselton Spence, M.Ed.: Reading Specialist, Greenwich, Connecticut; former elementary school principal in New York State. Coauthor of *Take Charge! Advocating for Your Child's Education* (2001).

Preface

This book is written for many different kinds of teachers, each with a different role to fulfill, each with a different skill and expertise. Each person's role plays an important part in striving for and creating more perceptive and effective learners. Each role is worthy of respect. Supervisors, teacher mentors, staff developers, educational administrators, directors of early childhood centers and nursery schools, and principals of early childhood programs in public, independent, and faith-based schools all know the various requirements of their work. It is not those differences that I will address, but rather the similarities which bind all of us together as a steadfast community of educators. It is this community, philosophically linked together, that believes that *together* we can make a difference in the life of each child that we touch. This book is for all of us.

Teaching is a gift . . . a gift for all persons in the field. Above all, teaching is an opportunity to create meaningful relationships with others. It is an opportunity to make a difference, to open new windows, open new doors, and allow rays of light to spill across a given space. Teaching is a thoughtful process . . . a process that calls for listening, observing, evaluating, and reflecting. It is a process that pleads for time and quiet and much introspection along the way. Teaching is more than just knowing: it is knowing and feeling in very close harmony. It calls for much understanding of how to best analyze and balance the two, and then to proceed with wisdom. Teaching is a gift, a gift to be unwrapped slowly over time. Teaching is a gift to enrich your life, so that you, in turn, can enrich the lives of others.

What binds us together has to do with how we present ourselves, our degree of dedication *and* humility. It has to do with the words that we choose and the inflection and tone of voice we use as we speak our well-chosen words. What binds us together is the knowledge of how important it is that we are good listeners, that we pay particular attention to individual differences and needs. What binds us together is our attention to detail, our knowledge that organization and follow-through are such important factors in being effective in our work. What binds us together is our yearning to be our best selves, our yearning to do the best possible work that we can. To be *role models* in everything we do and say, and also in what we don't do and don't say. How we comport ourselves is our common denominator. It defines our raison d'être. It personifies our profession.

Haim Ginott, in his classic work *Teacher and Child,* speaks about "congruent communication, where communication is harmonious, authentic; where words fit feelings" (1972, 81). He speaks about the importance of capturing a child's heart, feeling that "only if a child feels right can he think right." It is this same principle that I want to convey to all early childhood educators, so that they, in turn, can inspire the student teachers and teachers with whom they work to be genuine with children.

The word *genuine* carries along with it many beliefs . . . beliefs about honesty in whatever we say and do, beliefs about keeping our word, about being accountable for the work that we are certain needs to be done. Because we know that a child's self-respect, motivation, and attitude toward learning all have their beginnings in these early childhood years, it also carries with it the responsibility to see that good things happen to young children. Today we know how to create early childhood classrooms that are filled with materials that both allow and encourage exploration so that children can experience the delight in discovery. We want to see that each child has the opportunity to actualize his own potential and live out his dreams. Rachel Carson, in her monumental work *The Sense of Wonder*, wrote: "If a child is to keep alive his sense of wonder he needs the companionship of at least one adult who can share it, rediscovering with him the joy, excitement, and mystery of the world that we live in" (1956, 45). Let us pool our expertise and work together for those goals.

For the sake of clarity and ease in reading the text, I have chosen to speak about the mentoring process through the eyes and ears of a supervisor. In this case, the teachers-in-training are college students. All that is set forth here is, of course, applicable to all teachers-in-training. This includes new teachers, or more experienced ones, involved in the mentoring process who may not be affiliated with a college or university. Mentoring and supervision should ideally be done with the same spirit. Both look at the strengths of the teacher-in-training, with a view toward helping each teacher grow to his or her fullest potential. Mentoring, in whatever form it takes, should be based on a partnership created out of trust and collegiality. I have used the term *cooperating teacher* to designate the classroom teacher who works with the teachers-in-training on a daily basis. I fully recognize that both men and women hold all positions mentioned in the book. However, in order to simplify the text, I have attributed either male or female gender to each of the key players: The supervisor is female, the director or principal is male, and the cooperating teacher is female. The student teachers are both male and female. The term *student* always refers to the teacher-in-training here, and *children* is always used for the young learners in the classroom.

The Reasons for Writing the Book

My reasons for writing this book come from several deep convictions: (1) the belief that the supervision process is a collaborative effort, calling for the supervisor to work closely with the student teacher, the cooperating teacher, and, if possible, the director; (2) the belief that the supervisor can do the best possible job by joining the student teacher in the field placement classroom for extended periods of time; and (3) the belief that sharing thoughts and ideas through conferences, written observations, and journal responses creates a powerful form of communication. Together these convictions form the foundation for the supervision model.

The Book's Unique Features

The book's most unique feature is that it highlights the inclusion of the cooperating teacher as part of the supervision model. The cooperating teacher shares in the supervisor's written observations, the student's journal responses, and the conference time. This makes the supervision a truly collaborative effort, giving the student a substantial support system. The cooperating teacher's participation in the process greatly enhances the possibility of change within the classroom.

The book deals with everyday classroom issues, taken from my experience as a supervisor. Each chapter includes objectives, summaries, and reflective questions. Several chapters also include personal accounts. These are stories from the field—a supervisor's reflections.

The Organization of the Book

The book contains six chapters, a list of suggested readings, and three appendices. Chapter 1, "The Role of the Supervisor," describes what the primary strengths of the supervisor should be. This chapter also addresses some of the responsibilities that go along with the position. Chapter 2, "Great Expectations," looks into the student-supervisor relationship and how to work with the student teacher in the classroom. In Chapter 3, "What to Listen and Look for in the Learning Environment," I speak about what a supervisor should observe in an early childhood setting—and how this impacts the student teacher. Chapter 4, "Facilitating Student Learning," describes the student's responsibilities in dealing with both the classroom and written work. Chapter 5, "Handling the Challenging Issues," addresses various approaches for working alongside a resistant student, cooperating teacher, or director. Chapter 6, "Finding a Balance," describes how to put your work, including both the challenges and the successes, all into proper perspective.

The appendices include many pedagogical features: letters written to the student teacher and the cooperating teacher, observations, reflective journal responses, and evaluation forms. All information, except where otherwise noted, is gained firsthand from the author, except for two journal responses that were written by an esteemed colleague, Josephine Kellman.

The Art of Communication

Throughout my work, I have placed great emphasis on the art of communication and what it can mean in people's lives. I want to take the time to *listen* to what young children are saying. I also want to take the time to *listen* to what my students are saying. Listening helps me discover who these young people and students are. I like to take the time to *watch* how young children react to their peers and how they interact in their environment. Watching helps me understand the workings of their minds. I like to *watch* how my students react to other adult educators in the classroom and how they use the materials in the room. Watching my student teachers helps me understand the way they think. Taking the time to sit down with each of my students and *discuss* our shared experience, both on a philosophical and a practical level, brings us closer together and provides an opportunity for me to be supportive. All of this, in essence, is what I want my students to do with the children in the class. I want to model the art of communication and let my students know what a difference they can make in the lives of young children.

Acknowledgments

There is a Chinese proverb that says: "A journey begins with the first step." Writing a book is also a journey, albeit a solitary one. Yet my journey became greatly enhanced by the wisdom of friends and colleagues. Listening to *their* words has extended both the depth and breadth of the journey—and for that, I am ever grateful. I valued their time, support, and encouragement. Thank you, Jane Schoenberg, Carolyn Caselton Spence, Natalie R. Garfield, Melissa Heckler, and my dear mentor, Dr. JoAnn Shaheen. You were my guiding lights. My deep appreciation goes to Josephine Kellman, my esteemed colleague, and Sheila Hanna, Chair of Early Childhood at Westchester Community College, for believing in my work. My thanks to Jacalyn Rodriquez and Marcia Kingaton, two outstanding students at the college, whose work is included in the text, and Jennifer Davidson, for allowing me to use her son Dylan's story. And my heartfelt gratitude to my editor, Danny Miller. His enthusiasm for my work and clear vision have taken the revision process to an art form, filled with intelligence and esprit de corps.

The Role of the Supervisor

Objectives

After reading this chapter, you should understand

- the importance of establishing a caring student teacher–supervisor relationship;
- the importance of being flexible in order to accommodate the various learning styles of your students;
- what information you need to obtain about each student teacher for your own files;
- a number of ways to begin assessing the students' abilities within the classroom; and
- the role the supervisor can play as an agent of change.

Relationships are in large part what life is all about. Through these wondrous connections we become motivated to seek new heights, ask more of ourselves, and nurture our very beings. A student, in turn, responds in a positive manner within the context of a caring relationship. A student who feels at ease with a supervisor tends to discuss his uppermost concerns about his field placement work. So, from the very beginning, it is in everyone's best interest to build into the student teacher–supervisor relationship a high level of comfort and mutual respect. For the student, a high comfort level may include the freedom to question and discuss various ideas and activities that are at work in the classroom setting. A student should also be encouraged to question and discuss the ideas that the supervisor presents.

For the supervisor, the comfort level includes the freedom to question, discuss, and guide the student teacher toward greater self-awareness and fulfillment within the field of early childhood education. Over the semester the mutual respect grows as you work together, exchanging ideas and discussing why some things worked and others did not. You can use the classroom setting, which you both have shared, as the basis of your work together. With this as a context, you can ask the student questions: "How would you have handled the way Yi-Min refused to go to the end of the line after going down the slide?" or "How do you feel about Mohan spending all of his work time in the block area, never showing any interest in the art or science projects that are offered?" Spending time together creates the potential to foster and maintain a supportive relationship. Observation, conferences, written communication, critical thinking, and much reflection all fit together to form the foundation of the supervisory process.

Profiles of the Supervisor

Being a supervisor of college students of early childhood education offers many wonderful opportunities. Because the population of students is diverse in terms of age, ability, ethnicity, and learning style, there is a continual challenge to offer appropriate individual counseling. As an educator, you can revel in the image of what your diverse group of students can bring to many classrooms. Exposing young children to a variety of cultural traditions helps to crumble walls of discrimination and allow for a wider and clearer vision. Encourage your student teacher to share her special talents with the children—her singing and storytelling, her love of cooking favorite foods from her childhood. Let your student know that the pride in who she is may help young children feel that same emotion about themselves.

Mentoring Early Childhood Educators

You will want to give yourself as much time as you can to learn about your student. What are her particular family responsibilities at this stage in her life? Are there problems around her command of the English language? Are there any health issues that must be addressed? Does your student have learning problems? Whatever the degree of interest you show in your student, hopefully, this will be reflected in your student's interest in getting to know the children in her class.

Over the years I have found that one very successful method of getting to know each student teacher was to ask him to write me a paper titled "What I Would Like You to Know About Me." The paper was not mandatory. In order to best guide each of my students, I wanted to understand them as individuals, without being intrusive. Through each essay I learned about personal struggles, heartaches, and joys, which, in turn, allowed me to view each student with a deep respect for who he was. Each supervisor, knowing herself, must judge the extent of her emotional involvement with her students. However, it is imperative to always keep in mind her professional responsibilities to the field of early childhood education: to provide no less than the highest standards of training.

Being a supervisor calls for a keen sense of responsibility toward the student to support her efforts, struggles, and accomplishments throughout your time together. Hopefully, you will have had many years of experience in the field, including being a classroom teacher, and thus will be able to speak from your own personal experience. Just as classroom teachers try to understand each child's likes, dislikes, sensitivities, special abilities, and disabilities, so must you strive to know your student teacher and her unique qualities as an individual learner.

Having the chance to work one-on-one with an aspiring teacher is a notable opportunity. It is particularly valuable in today's hurried world, where many people feel pressed for time, always having to move quickly to meet the next appointment on their schedule. The student-supervisor relationship strives to be an unpressured and sustaining force for the teacher-in-training. The most important factor for the supervisor is the expectation that she enter into these personal and academic relationships with an open mind and a deep caring for the welfare and growth of each student.

It is appropriate for you, the supervisor, to present yourself in a professional manner, to be neatly dressed and have your papers well organized. It is helpful to have a separate file folder for each student teacher with her name correctly spelled on the tab. Each folder should hold an information card with the essential information about the student's whereabouts that keeps you and the student well connected. In addition you can request that the student provide very specific written directions (turn left at the Sunoco station) on the back of the card to guide you to her job site. See below for information that should be requested on the card.

Upon entering any new center, it is imperative, for reasons of security, to always present yourself at the office, introduce yourself, and obtain permission to visit your student. Once you have arrived in the classroom, it is important to greet Juanita, your student, and meet the cooperating and assistant teachers. If class is already in session, then these formalities can be deferred to a later time. The thrust of the moment is to settle yourself as quickly and as unobtrusively as possible and begin to take in the climate of this particular room. How does it feel to be there? Are the children moving freely from one activity to another, or are they required to sit quietly until the teacher directs them to the next activity? How do the adults manage their

Name:	
Name of Center/School:	
Address of Center/School:	
Phone Number of Center/School:	
Director:	
Cooperating Teacher:	
Room Number:	
Days and Hours of Work:	
Home Address:	
Home Telephone:	Cell Phone (optional):
Email Address:	Fax Number:

Mentoring Early Childhood Educators

time in terms of being available to the children, and most importantly, what is Juanita doing?

What Does the Supervisor Look and Listen For?

As a supervisor it is important to be unhurried. You want Juanita to know that you are there to focus on her and the quality of her interactions. How often does she ask questions in order to clarify what needs to be done? Observe the way she watches the other teachers in the room to determine how deeply she is invested in the teaching process. You should be eager to focus on her interactions with the children as well. You will want to watch the way she moves and see how quickly she responds to any given situation. Does Juanita move from one group to another, happily involving herself in different play situations, or does she get stuck, unsure of how to move on? Does she pick an appropriate spot to read *Gilberto and the Wind*, which Seth has requested, so that there is room for others to join them if they so choose? Does Juanita willingly bundle up to join the class on the playground, even though the temperature is low? Does she keep a watchful eye on the children outside instead of huddling together with the other adults who are engaged in social banter? Does she put forth the same interest in observing and interacting with young children outside as she has shown inside the classroom?

Categories of Competency

Body Language

You will want to pay attention to Juanita's body language. Is she attentive, smiling, and very present, or does she sit back and wait for things to happen around her? You will want to know how much physical contact she has with Bianca and Trevor. Is Juanita at ease taking Trevor on her lap to comfort him after a difficult Monday-morning separation from his mom? Does she feel comfortable giving a hug, if a hug seems called for, after Bianca bangs her finger at the workbench? Will Juanita move a puzzle out of the way if it has been left on the floor in the line of traffic? Will she mop up some snow that has been brought in on the children's boots, without being asked, before someone takes a spill? Will she move alongside Antonio if he is having difficulty staying quiet at story time? Does Juanita usually have a smile on her face, indicating that she takes great pleasure in being in the company of young children?

Language

It is important to listen to the student teacher's words, not only for what she says, but also for what she doesn't say, as well as the inflections and tonality of her voice. Is Juanita soft-spoken and patient, or is she sometimes demanding and accusatory? Does she speak to children respectfully and then give them all the time they need to say what is on their minds? Does she express herself in simple words that the children will easily understand? Will she repeat a sentence a child has said using correct English, rather than tell Colin that he made a mistake? Will she take Natasha aside, to ensure privacy, and talk quietly with her if she has something very personal to share? Is Juanita specific with her praise instead of just saying, "Good job"? Has she learned each child's name and how to pronounce it just the way the child wants it pronounced? Does she listen to the way the cooperating teacher uses language and try to incorporate some of those phrases into her own vocabulary? Does she enthusiastically join in the children's singing or teach them a new verse to "The Garden Song"? Does she take on the two different voices of Frog and Toad when she reads the story *Frog and Toad Are Friends*? Is she able to project her voice in order to gain the attention of the group?

Group Management

You will want to observe if Juanita is able to keep an eye on everyone in the class, even though she is playing Farm Lotto with only four children. How capable is she in pinpointing trouble spots? Does she hear and respond to the rising decibel level of Shaniqua's voice from the block corner and then move in that direction? Is she aware that Oona has been sitting very quietly by herself with her head resting on the table? Will she draw up a chair in the pretend area and have

Mentoring Early Childhood Educators

Omar style her hair at Walt's Barber Shop? How does she react when Lucas, Nina, and Suzanne all want her to sit next to them at snack? Is it hard for her to say, "No, I cannot allow you to do that," when Hendrik kicks Josh's block building and it crashes to the floor? Notice if she seeks to work only with individual children or if she looks comfortable working with larger groups. Does Juanita shy away from a flare-up that could call for conflict resolution? Is she a good anticipator? Do children listen to what she has to say? Does she seize the teachable moment?

The Supervisor as an Agent of Change

A supervisor has the opportunity to act as an agent of change within each center or school where she works. Each student and each cooperating teacher has the potential to influence the lives of children, now and for the future. Sitting down with one another as colleagues, sharing ideas in an open and free-flowing way, often leads to an invitation for you to offer some of your thoughts. During these times you can make it clear that your words are to be taken only in the light of "things to think about and talk about among yourselves." Ideas are exchanged in the general spirit of improving the overall learning environment, and specifically in offering the possibility of a new approach or new way of looking at an existing problem. Within this framework, coming together can become a relaxed, meaningful, and often productive time. The thrust of working together is to learn from one another.

Imagine you have just spent the morning in a classroom full of four-year-olds. It appeared to you that there were problems in making the transition from work time to snack time. Many of the children simply went on doing whatever they had been doing after the teacher said, "It's time to clean up." Naiyana and Mark went right on building with blocks, Zachary sat comfortably reading *Harry the Dirty Dog*, and Pippi and Mary Jane continued to push around a shopping cart, still adorned in high heels and long skirts. The teachers spent most of their time asking Zachary, Pippi, and the others to put this away here or that away there. In conversation at conference time, after the class has ended, you might lead into the subject by asking the cooperating teacher and your student, "How did you feel the cleanup time went today?" This type of question can often bring forth sighs, moans, declarations of frustration—and much discussion. Further into the conversation, at an appropriate moment, you might ask, "Would you consider singing a short rhyme like 'Five more minutes left to play; time to put the toys away'?" This, or some other animated expectation, could be used to build in a greater definition and bridge between the two activities. These words could help the children gain a greater awareness of how they need to structure their remaining work time in order to put the finishing touches on the blocks or check out the groceries from the store. Perhaps there will be the right opportunity to ask, "What do you think about the idea of getting children more involved in the cleanup process by asking them to select their own jobs?" These pivotal questions can become pathways to an even more in-depth discussion. However, whether the timing is right for posing such questions is a critical decision that only you, the skilled supervisor, can make.

In my four-year-old classroom, the excitement that was engendered by cleanup time was something to behold. Whether it was brought on by the children's sense of pride in and ownership of their own room or by the anticipation of a delicious snack was never really determined, but it was an important part of our day. I had an old autoharp that I used to strum as I moved around the room, kneeling in front of each child and singing, "What would you like to do today, what would you like to put away?" (I did this after I had given the children a five-minute warning.) I never felt that it was necessary for a child to clean up where she played; rather, I wanted each child to understand the larger concept of teachers and children working together in a community effort. Cleanup time was just as exhilarating as work time!

Another possible topic for a conference discussion is room arrangement, which often is given little thought after the initial setup of the room is done. Sometimes simple changes in the placement of furniture can allow children to use a particular space in an alternative or expanded way. In one child care center, there were up to twenty children in a rather small room. The left-hand side of the room contained a large pretend area and a small portion of space

Mentoring Early Childhood Educators

that was allocated for blocks. The positioning of the block shelf allowed for an area of only approximately two feet by four feet for building. Adjacent to that area was a table where the children sat to eat their breakfast. After spending the morning there and observing the quality of the play, you could pose the question: "What are your feelings about the activity that went on in the block area this morning?" If you have already established a good working relationship with the cooperating teacher and your student, you might ask, "Did you feel Ian, Richard, and Byung were getting in each other's way, despite their trying hard to build a swimming pool together?" After the three of you explore the subject, you might touch on the frustration the children must have felt while trying to retrieve more blocks from the shelf without knocking down part of their work. Here again, when the timing seems appropriate, you could offer the following thought: "Would you consider the possibility of moving the block shelf back three or four feet to enlarge the area for block play and reduce the size of the pretend area?" You could explain that this would give the children a much larger area in which to work and be out of the traffic pattern as their classmates come to sit down for breakfast. As the conversation proceeds you can constantly weigh how animated and receptive the cooperating teacher and Juanita are. You can make decisions as you talk about the amount of additional material you want to include. Should you mention the need to always have the block shelf look orderly and inviting. Yes! Should you mention the need to have accessories, including hard hats, right on top of the block shelf, or should this wait for a later date? It is your choice. You also have the option of looking at your work through a wide-angle lens. Even if your "thoughts to consider" are not incorporated into the program this year, there is always the possibility that the cooperating teacher or the student teacher will begin the following year with some of these new concepts or approaches set firmly in place.

Change can come about in small ways and can come about gradually as well. Sometimes it is the shift of something tangible—a shelf, a table, a chair, or even the removal of a rusty gym locker. Whatever the change, it can make a difference in how the children use the space and how they feel about their play. Change can come about in the way a word or phrase is spoken or in a new way to regard a child. However small the change may be, it is the repositioning that opens up a space for new insights to emerge.

As a supervisor you want to be there in all the ways that you can, knowing each student through her actions and reactions. You want to read the expression on her face and, thus, fine-tune your own perceptions. You want to know how she thinks and what thoughts guide her to make the decisions that she makes, by walking along the thought processes of her mind. You want to discuss all this in an open and honest way, so she will know that you are available and there for her. These are the important things you bring as you walk into a center.

Summary

Supervision is the art of working closely with students and teachers as colleagues, supporting one another in a quest for greater self-knowledge and knowledge in a chosen field. It is presenting yourself as an organized person, intent upon watching, listening, and recording the sights and sounds of the classroom. It is sharing observations as "thoughts to consider" in bringing forth an improved climate of learning within any given classroom—and being appreciative of the opportunity of just being there.

Reflective Questions

1. Can you think of additional ways to put your student teacher more at ease?

2. What other questions would help you evaluate your student's performance?

3. If you feel conflicted about talking to both the student and the cooperating teacher at the same time, what measures can you take to increase your own comfort?

4. Considering your degree of commitment, as well as your own schedule, how much time can you realistically give to observe your student in the classroom?

5. What struggles do you have in drawing and maintaining the fine line between responsibilities to yourself and responsibilities to your student? Do your empathy and involvement allow you to keep your focus on the student's work?

Great Expectations—
Enter . . . the Students

Objectives

After reading this chapter, you should understand

- that the quality of the student teacher–supervisor relationship is a key factor in the supervision process;
- a number of ways to get to know the student that could help to put him at ease;
- how broad a spectrum the role of note taking can cover;
- where to best position yourself in the classroom for observation and recording;
- how to structure a conference that includes the cooperating teacher; and
- what important factors to include in the written observation.

Being a college student (or a teacher-in-training) is an enviable position. The concentration of one's efforts are on inquiry, investigation, and reflection. A student is supported in many ways, not unlike a young child who is cradled, nurtured, and protected. A student is allowed freedom and granted leeway in his actions. Educators who surround a student are patient; they offer their advice because students are people who are prized. Part of what propels a student to learn is the atmosphere that surrounds him. Educators want each student to succeed, to become the best person and teacher that he can be. These expectations deserve respect.

The Student-Supervisor Relationship

Before you actually meet your student, if you can, take the time to send him a handwritten letter or email. If this isn't practical, you might talk with him on the telephone. You will want the student to know that you are reaching out to him. You will want Terry, the student, to know that you are a caring individual, both approachable and communicative. You will want him to know that you enter into this relationship with anticipation, enthusiasm, and a sense of adventure. Here are two sample letters that could be sent to students:

September 1

Dear Bjorn:

I have just received your name from the college. I will be your supervisor for the Early Childhood Field Experience course at Ripton Community College.

I wanted you to know that I am looking forward to working with you, and to the journey that we will be taking together, as you work with children and staff at the Hawthorn School. Please feel free to call me with any questions. My home phone number is 555/586-6990. I plan to visit Professor Shaheen's Early Childhood Curriculum class on Monday, September 9, at 3:00 P.M. At that time I will have the opportunity to meet you in person. I look forward to that.

Best regards,
Kathryn Reed

September 9

Dear Mira:

Hello, let me introduce myself. My name is Sara Kate Williams and I will supervise your practicum work at South Orange Child Care Center. I would like to visit you within the next two weeks. Please check your calendar, clear your choice of dates with your cooperating teacher, and call me. My phone number at the college is 555/997-2434, extension 4. I look forward to hearing from you.

Sincerely,
Sara Kate Williams

Meeting the Student

If you do not already have your student in class, try to meet him in advance of the first site visit. It seems to relieve a certain amount of his anxiety. This meeting can also give you the opportunity to say a few words about your style of observation, the length of your stay in the classroom, and what you see as your role once you are in the classroom. At this time, you can request each student to ask the co-operating teacher, well in advance, what days would be convenient for her to have you observe.

If you are a visual person, you may, after seeking permission from Terry, take a snapshot of him that will go in his file folder. You will want to learn each of your students' names right away, and having a picture gives you the opportunity to quiz yourself when your time allows.

Perhaps the most important part of your meeting is to have empathy with the student teacher. The field placement will be, for many, a first experience in a leadership role in the classroom. Entering an unfamiliar environment carries with it a mixture of emotions—both an eager anticipation and an uneasiness of not knowing what to expect. A student might feel that he will be expected to know what his role is as a team member . . . but this is not possible at this point in time. You will want to allay his fears. Let Terry understand that a field placement is an opportunity for learning and should be looked upon as an extension of the college classroom. Here, at long last, the student teacher has an arena to put theory into practice. He can see first-hand how the cooperating teacher works with a large group of children. He can see the reactions that children have to the words that he has chosen to say. Being in the classroom is the culmination of all the reading, writing, and discussion that has gone on before with the course work. However, just like many things, the experience should be entered into thoughtfully and taken day by day. It should be a time when the student can both feel free to ask questions and take the time to reflect upon each day's happenings. You may suggest that the student keep a list of questions about situations that puzzle him or a particular child who interests him. Any question that Terry might have is worthy of your earnest consideration and discussion.

Whether or not an answer is forthcoming is not as significant as the fact that you address and reflect upon the question. If you can, recall and share how you felt on your first day as a student teacher. Let him know how overwhelmed you felt as you watched Ms. Miller make decision after decision on how to manage twenty-one five-year-olds with what seemed like the wisdom of the ages. It could also be helpful to introduce the concept that there is no right way to tackle each problem, that every situation warrants its own scrutiny and judgment. You may also want to emphasize that you, like every student, learn through your own experiences—and that no one is expected to do a perfect job. The best that you can do for Terry is to try to put his student teaching experience into perspective, so that he will feel less apprehensive and more at ease.

The Role of Note Taking

One of the hurdles that you must cross is conveying that note taking is part and parcel of the supervision process. You want Terry to understand that your note taking is intended to help you recall as much as you can about a particular environment and the people within that setting. You may want to take notes about what is hanging on the walls, how the manipulatives are labeled and kept, how fresh and inviting the paints and easel look, and how well marked and orderly the block shelves are. Look and see if the snack has been set up in advance, so that children do not have to sit and wait too long. If there are animals in the classroom, you may wish to observe how they are cared for and by whom. Try to see if the dress-up clothes are attractively displayed on hooks or hangers or if they are stuffed helter-skelter into a covered toy chest, completely out of sight. You want each student to understand that all the notes you take are not just about him. You are trying to take in the total picture of the climate of this particular room. Of course, a good proportion of your notes will be about Terry. If you can, try to record specific conversations and the reactions from both the children and your student. Watch for the ease, or lack of ease, with which children handle transitions and how helpful Terry is in this process. You may want to pay particular attention to how disciplinary problems are handled and how involved your student is in this process. Has he noticed Chai, a quiet child, who may be just outside the ring of excitement in the class? How does he react when Mario, an acting-out child, interrupts a group discussion by clowning? Try to see what Terry is seeing and how he chooses to spend his time. You will want your student to know all this in advance, to know that this is how you see your job and what you need to do.

Position Is Everything

You may also tell your student that you will sit quietly within the room, positioning yourself so that you can see and hear as much as possible. Try to stay in close proximity to Terry so that you can hear the quality of interaction that is taking place. At times, this can mean moving your chair once or twice during a morning or afternoon visit, though you may prefer to remain still. Since you want to see the class in as normal a situation as possible, you may consider not initiating any conversations with the children, even though the temptation is enormous. If a child asks a question like, "Are you Terry's sister?" then it is certainly appropriate to give a short explanation of who you are.

Paving the Way

You will need to tell your student that it is his responsibility to inform the cooperating teacher and the director of the date and time of arrival for each of your visits. Ideally, the children should also be told in advance that a visitor is coming, and just who that person is. Letting children in on what goes on in their classroom is a way of showing them respect. Perhaps you have had the experience of being handed a four-inch square of oak tag and asked to write down what you wanted the children to call you—and then later being introduced at group time. Some cooperating teachers have reflected upon how to welcome and incorporate a visitor into a classroom in a very thoughtful way.

Many years ago, when I was a graduate student at Bank Street College of Education in New York City, our group visited a well-known therapeutic nursery school in the city. Before our observation, we were taken into a room adjacent to the nursery, which had a one-way mirror. The instructions were: "Absolutely no interaction with teachers, therapists, parents, or children. Just sit quietly, period. No eye contact, no smiling, just sit quietly until after all the children have gone." I remember it all so vividly. I was seated in a small chair to the side of the entrance/exit in the nursery room. There were only half a dozen children in the room and an equal number of teachers and therapists. The morning session was coming to a close. Parents came, one by one, to pick up their children. Carlos had just put his jacket on and was headed, with his mom, past me and toward the door. As he approached, he slapped me across the face with a stinging and resounding blow. To say the least, I was stunned, but far more important than the momentary reaction was the profound and lasting effect that episode had on me. Simply because I was there, I was an intrusion. I have taken heed of Carlos' message. I want to always be deeply aware of what my presence can mean within any given room to any given child, whose inner life can be only briefly glimpsed. In this particular situation perhaps our instructions were not thought through carefully enough. Perhaps it would have been better to let us remain behind the one-way mirror.

How to Facilitate a Conference

An integral part of the supervision process is to have *sufficient* conference time with your student after the visit to the classroom. The conference can take place within the classroom if the children have gone to the playground or to the cafeteria for lunch. If the room itself is not available, then an unused office or kitchen can be utilized—wherever you can be comfortable and private. The talking together can last up to an hour. Generally, however, you may find it will be closer to thirty minutes, depending upon the student's needs and availability or upon your concerns or time constraints. You may be surprised to find that during your first time together, Terry may open up and talk with you not only about his present placement but also about plans for his future professional life.

If at all possible, invite the cooperating teacher to sit and join you when you talk. Very often you may find that the invitation alone casts a whole different light on your presence in the classroom and all the ensuing interactions. You may also see that it brings a broad smile to the cooperating teacher's face. The invitation immediately conveys respect for her ability as a teacher and the work she is doing in the student's behalf. Above all, it acknowledges that the two of you are colleagues, working together in a *joint* effort to move Terry forward from student to teacher.

Of course, each conference will be different, but you may find an underlying format could prove helpful in structuring the proceedings. Because you are a visitor, it is well to thank the cooperating teacher for the opportunity of being in the room. Begin with a number of positive statements about the general climate of the room: "It is rewarding to see the children deeply invested in their work" or "Having each adult work with half of the group at a time allows for so much more individual attention." You may also want to comment on the general appearance of the room: "Using children's artwork to decorate the walls gives the children such a sense of pride in the value of their work" or "It's always exciting to see seedlings being started by the windows—a real promise of spring." Any of these comments acts as an opening statement for more in-depth discussion. Then, you may want to ask how each person feels about how the morning or afternoon went. Question whether it seemed like a normal day, or if your presence made a big difference. If either the cooperating teacher or Terry feels that your being there made it very atypical, then you could ask for suggestions. Could you sit in another spot? Was your note taking distracting? What could you do to make the situation more comfortable for all concerned?

Because the three of you have been at the same place at the same time, you have common ground from which to work. Together you can consider other alternatives to Jose's mutinous stance at cleanup time. You can put your heads together to think about Charlotte's extraordinary ability in making paper animals and how she might use her talent to extend her social relationships. Together you can explore why there was no block building going on for this group of

Mentoring Early Childhood Educators

four-year-olds. You can also have a dialogue about the next unit of study, on gardening. You could brainstorm about the organization and infinite possibilities that this engaging subject can hold.

There should also be time for questioning Terry about his satisfactions and concerns in the classroom. What does he find rewarding or perplexing? Does he feel as though he is being challenged to stretch his mind and broaden his horizons? Does he feel overwhelmed about the responsibility of caring for other people's children? If you sense that there is a good working relationship between Terry and the cooperating teacher, you should certainly acknowledge the meaningfulness of this. If, on the other hand, you sense a strain between the two, you can always talk privately to either one and work to resolve the issues. Perhaps Terry is not taking his responsibilities to heart and is arriving half an hour late each day. Perhaps the cooperating teacher has not taken the time to sit and talk with Terry and give him the direction he craves.

A conference time is also a time for doing some long-range planning about the next steps for Terry in assuming a greater role in small-group management. You will want to explain how important it is for him to plan and set up activities on his own. By doing this, Terry can more fully understand what is encompassed in running a classroom. Because you are working as a team, equally sharing your ideas, the possibility that changes will be made is greatly increased. Asking the questions, "What do you think about . . . ?" and "What has your experience been?" is helpful in keeping the conversation in balance.

At the end of the conference, go over the dates and times of the rest of your visits. Put the dates right into your calendar and give Terry a completed form with the same information for him to keep. This form should include phone numbers and addresses where you can be reached throughout the year. (See Figure 2–1.)

Part of the goal of the conference is trying to raise Terry's consciousness and develop his critical eye. You want the student to think, "How could I have handled the situation better?" or "How could I have extended the play?" Perhaps he will question himself: "Could I have more effectively helped Rachel work through her feelings of remorse after she snatched the diamond necklace from around Samantha's neck?" With every issue raised, the student teacher has the opportunity to move forward in developing an

Figure 2–1

Appointment Sheet

Dear _____,

I will be your fieldwork supervisor for the Early Childhood Field Experience course. I am pleased that we will have the opportunity of working together on an individual basis.

I will be visiting you at your site on the following dates:

Date: _____ A.M. _____ P.M. _____

Date: _____ A.M. _____ P.M. _____

Date: _____ A.M. _____ P.M. _____

Please be certain to have your journal material with you. It is important to notify your cooperating teacher and director of the dates and times of my visits. If you will not be present on that day, please call and leave a message on my answering machine as soon as you are aware of a conflict. If it is a last-minute problem, please call me before 7:30 A.M.

MY PHONE NUMBERS:	555/586-6990 (home)
	555/997-2434, extension 4 (work)
	555/586-6680 (cell)
MY ADDRESS:	333 Applewood Lane
	Troy, NY 48098
MY EMAIL ADDRESS:	carolbhillman67@yahoo.com
MY FAX NUMBER:	555/586-9053

I look forward to hearing from you.

Sincerely,
Carol Hillman

expanded consciousness and gaining a more critical eye. The supervisor-student dialogue, grounded in mutual respect, is the model you want your student to mirror with the children in his classroom.

The Written Observation

The written observation that you give or send to the student teacher and the cooperating teacher is the tangible result of the site visit and the conference that the three of you have shared.

Writing to both the student and the cooperating teacher and including the cooperating teacher in the collaborative process was a long-considered and difficult professional decision to make. Through the years it has proven to be the quintessential element in the success of this supervision model. Including the cooperating teacher in all forms of communication sets the tone of our work together. It establishes, from the very beginning, that we play equally important roles in the process of training the student. I think, more than anything, it validates my respect for the daily work that the cooperating teacher has been doing and will continue to do throughout the year. It dispels any possible notion that a supervisor or mentor holds a loftier position. It puts us on the same plane . . . as colleagues. However, it is not without its difficulties. Some confidentiality must be gently brushed aside in order to attain the larger benefit of open communication. Because I am including the cooperating teacher in my written observation, it makes me consider each sentence more thoughtfully. I think about how my remarks might impact upon the student–cooperating teacher relationship. I think about the importance of maintaining the cooperating teacher's sense of her own professionalism. I have some concerns about the constraints it may impose on my student's openness in discussion. Once again, it reminds me that I am an outsider looking in, that this is not my classroom.

In each written observation you may consider doing the following:

- addressing the observation first to the student and then to the cooperating teacher (Coteachers and assistant teachers can also be included.)

- dating the observation and noting the visit number (visit 1, 2, or 3)
- thanking the cooperating teacher for welcoming you into the classroom
- beginning with positive comments about the general climate and environment of the room, involvement of the children, spaciousness, room arrangement, and so on
- outlining briefly that the observation may include comments on
    - equipment and usage
    - curriculum
    - group time
    - transitions
    - student interaction with children
    - student initiative, creativity, leadership, questions, or suggestions
- ending with a positive comment
- including a reminder of the date and time of the next appointment
- thanking both the student and the cooperating teacher for their cooperation in your final observation
- offering to be available to both the student and the cooperating teacher if you can be of help to them in the future

Following are two sample observations:

February 1   Visit #1

Rosa and Eddie,

Thank you for welcoming me to your center and showing me around. I was so pleased to see how comfortable you are in your surroundings. You appear very "at home" with the children and the room that you all share. You have a presence about you that both is calm and gives off the feeling that everything is under control. This is very reassuring to young children, and it usually comes only after many years of experience. It's great that you are there.

Let me start out by giving you some overall impressions of the room and what I observed. Then I'll discuss some specific details relating to interactions with the children.

First of all, the room is filled with light and color. One is immediately struck with the upbeat quality of the furnishings, as well as the "fresh" look of the room. I am, however, puzzled by the size (small) of the tables and chairs, being that this is a mixed-age group. It somehow seems to me that it would be more respectful of the older children, the Pauls and B.J.s, if they had more suitable furniture for their size. I saw clear plastic bins that were marked with pictures of what they contained. This seemed so appropriate. Could the words *art gallery* and *writing center* also be represented in pictures?

I was delighted by the quality of the block play that I observed. So much involvement. Hugh doing "the parts of the house," even though he wasn't sure what they were. Two others were making a stove, cooking and flipping hamburgers. B.J. was working so hard at hammering. It was wonderful. And you, Rosa, are a very aware caregiver, extending the play in so many ways through questions, comments, and actually bringing props to the play area. You asked questions like: "What do you need for your house?" and "What are you going to have for dinner?" Bringing cups and skillets for the kitchen and hats for the closet were very indicative of your understanding and valuing the play of young children. I also observed that if part of the "wall" fell over, you put it back in place so as not to interrupt the flow of the play. Did you know that B.J. had a "flashlight" (a cylinder block) stuck in his pocket? Added protection in the house!

Now, let's jump from all this wonderful, stimulating play to the larger framework of the morning's activities, recognizing all the while the children's deep commitment to their work. To begin with, the primary focus is providing the best possible environment for young children, in which they can grow to their fullest potential. A simple statement, yet we all know this is a complex issue that involves deep thought and constant re-evaluation. Let me offer some thoughts for the two of you to discuss and reflect upon: How would you feel about having all the centers open at all times? Having all the centers open at all times makes the classroom more homey. It also helps children in the decision-making process. As it turned out, the pretend area, although closed, was irresistible to a number of children, as well as to Paul's special ed teacher. Having greater availability to the centers increases the possibility of more spontaneous and creative play.

Would you consider letting each child be the judge of how long he or she stays in a center? The reason I mention this is because it is hard for a child to have a time limit imposed from the outside. A child can be in the beginning, the middle, or the end of his or her work plan. This may not be apparent to an adult. When is a block building completed? When is a painting finished? These are individual determinations of the architect and the artist, and ten to fifteen minutes at a given place may just not be long enough.

Since it is so popular, what would you think about enlarging the block area? Could the large trucks be removed completely? Could they be used in the large motor area just outside the room? Could the piece with bins of manipulatives find a new home elsewhere in the room? Could the shelf on the right, as you enter the block area, be moved back toward the science area to allow for more floor space?

Rosa, when you call the children to line up to go to the playground, grab that teachable moment. Make it fun—"Anyone with pink shoelaces," or "Anyone with blue eyes," head for the door.

Keep up the good work, Rosa. You are a natural teacher, and I welcome the opportunity of working with you.

Carol

March 21   Visit #2

Carlen and Ria,

Carlen has told me that you will soon be leaving your position as lead teacher at Maple Grove, Ria. I want to extend my good wishes to you in your new work and also thank you for your cooperation in allowing Carlen to participate so much in working with the children in the classroom.

Carlen, we talked after class about the box collage project, which I feel was a great success in the eyes of the children. It was creative, open-ended, and challenging. The children had to tackle problems of design, balance, and choice of materials to attain their goals. The project allowed children to work cooperatively as well. It is certainly worth a repeat performance, as it was very popular with the children. Here are a few things to think about that might make the project easier the next go-round. Would you consider working at a table with the corrugated base placed in the center of the table, which has been covered with newspaper? I think it would be an advantage to have the chairs removed from around the table so that the children could walk around the "box building" while deciding where they want to place their box. If available, see if you could use Elmer's glue, as it dries clear. Also, *washable* magic markers are the marker of choice for young children. With the project on the table, you could place scissors, glue, and tape around the table at various locations. You could display the boxes themselves on top of the block shelf. In that way, the children could see the full range of their choices. In advance of the project, you could ask each child to collect at least three boxes and bring them to school. This way, you are creating interest even before they start to work. Be sure that you have a piece of corrugated large enough to accommodate their wildest dreams! It would be nice, as you suggested, to document the whole process next time, from your first discussion with the children as to what type of boxes they might have at their home, to a story about what they made. Keep a record of conversations, take photographs, and perhaps have the children, collectively, both talk about and draw their plans. You may even want to add a second or third day of building before painting, depending on how involved the children have become in their work.

I noted that Willie cut himself with a metal cookie cutter. There are two options: (1) to remove all metal cookie cutters and replace them with plastic ones or (2) to talk with the children at group time, explaining what happened (and how), and let them learn how to handle the cutters that you have. I am reminded about something that I saw in Reggio Emilia, Italy, when I was there. Young four-year-olds were working with broken pieces of glass, doing a mosaic of sorts. My initial reaction was one of horror. I had always taken great pains not to have anything glass in the classroom . . . just in case. Seeing what the children did at Reggio opened up a new door for me. My feeling has been, from that time forward, give the child or children the opportunity to learn how to handle materials properly and respect those materials. The children, thus entrusted with this responsibility, will rise to the occasion.

Carlen, we also spoke about having a dictionary in the room. It is such a wonderful tool for learning, not only how to spell a word, but also for children to see that learning is an ongoing process.

We spoke about David's visit/interview. How important it is for the child's family to understand the process of separation and what a parent's or grandparent's role is in this procedure. This is a far-reaching issue, and I hope that it is addressed in advance of the time that the children begin their stay at Maple Grove. Your taking a picture of David and the children that were in the room with him was a sensational idea! It made his leave-taking so much easier.

One other thing that I want to mention is the use of the word *we*, as in "Could we walk in the classroom?" or "What happens when a jacket is on the floor—what do we have to do?" Children know that teachers don't run in the classroom and they pick up their own jacket if it falls to the ground. What we are really saying to children is that what they are doing is not appropriate behavior. This can be translated into: "It would be better if you could walk in the classroom; running is not a safe thing to do" or "Each child is expected to pick up his or her own jacket and put it where it belongs." These statements or similar phrases are much more direct and powerful than the use of *we*.

Nice to see the children setting the snack table. What would you think about the addition of a two-cup measure so that they could pour their own juice and also be learning about ounces and cups at the same time?

Hope you will be doing some indoor/outdoor planting, now that spring is officially here. Please share this with Kristy and Li Li. I look forward to my next visit on Friday, April 27, at 9:00 A.M.

Carol

Summary

As a supervisor, you are facilitating a new student–cooperating teacher relationship. Give yourself time to write, email, or phone your student in advance of meeting him before the first site visit. When you meet your student, explain the role of note taking and how you will position yourself within the room. Ask your student to tell the cooperating teacher, director, and children when you are coming to visit. You will want to give yourself ample time to conference with the student and the cooperating teacher after the visit. Leave a written form with your student with the dates and times of future visits. After you have reflected upon your shared experiences, send your student and the cooperating teacher a detailed written observation of your time together—and look forward to the next visit!

Reflective Questions

1. How can you best present yourself to a new student teacher?

2. What humorous or poignant episodes that happened to you as a student teacher can you recall and share with your student?

3. What could you include on a checklist for note taking that could be helpful to you?

4. What topics can you think of that would make a three-way conference extremely difficult? How would you approach resolving these issues?

What to Listen and Look for in the Learning Environment

Objectives

After reading this chapter, you should understand

- how a mixture of different elements creates the climate of a classroom;
- what to listen and look for within the classroom;
- how room arrangement impacts the curriculum and comfort of the children;
- what significance group times can have within the program;
- children's need to move from one activity area to another, without a time restriction;
- the necessity of having all activity centers open at all times;
- what to expect to see within different activity areas;
- how the teacher sets the stage for play; and
- the role of project work in building a community of learners.

Thirty-seven years ago I purchased a farm among the hills of western Massachusetts. The house, an old saltbox, was built in 1750. It had been neglected for decades and stood vacant for four years. An acacia tree pressed dangerously against the southeast corner and had to be taken down. The foundation needed shoring up, so deep trenches had to be dug, and large mounds of earth covered the back yard. Asphalt shingles had to be removed so cedar shakes could be put in their place. Interior ceilings and walls had to be replastered. Warped floorboards had to be replaced; paint and wallpaper had to be stripped from the walls. The place was a mess. Amidst all this chaos, my mother came east from Kansas City. She carried plastic shopping bags filled with crimson phlox, white iris, and blackberry lilies. We set about to make a garden. The garden, designed in the shape of a crescent moon, duplicates the form of the rolling hills in the background, which overlook the Quabbin reservoir. The phlox were given center stage while the white iris and blackberry lilies graced each side—and so the garden began. Soon the trenches became filled in, and soft hay-scented ferns were dug into the earth all along the back of the house. The interior walls and ceilings have all been restored; the warped floorboards have been replaced; the mellowness of the old wood panels has been uncovered. The old house has reclaimed its past.

I have, as long as I can remember, been interested in environments, not only in creating a beautiful place wherever I may be but also in appreciating what others do to create aesthetic pleasure within a given site. What I see and feel about a place plays upon my very being and makes my heart sing in major or minor chords.

And so it is, as a supervisor of early childhood students in early childhood settings, that I look for, and oftentimes find, the same sense of loveliness within a given classroom. Here, children and teachers are working together to create visual, social, and intellectual harmony . . . a kind of inner garden.

A Classroom for All Seasons

The climate of a classroom is the sum total of many parts, both tangible and intangible. It has to do with many factors for which there is no scientific formula. There are aesthetics, philosophy, knowledge, hard work, and love served up in different portions. There are no absolutes that determine a perfect learning environment, therefore, I offer the following *guidelines*.

Figure 3–1

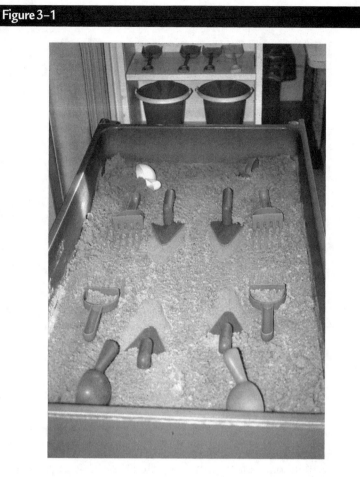

Stop—Listen and Look

Close your eyes and listen for the sounds of the room. Are there animated conversations going on among the children? Do the cooperating teacher and her assistant talk with the children in lively but well-modulated voices? Is a record playing "Baby Beluga" in the background? Is there the sound of blocks being stacked one upon another, as a small group of children build an airport? Is there water running in the sink where Kimberly and Myshawn are whipping up a bowl full of Ivory Snow, pretending to make their favorite chicken

Figure 3–2

noodle soup? Do you hear the soft squeals of Marmalade, the class guinea pig, as he nibbles a carrot in pure delight? Do you hear the click-clack of a pair of high-heeled silver party shoes as Joleen sashays across the vinyl tile floor? Can you detect the pounding of a roofing nail piercing a brass-plated canning jar lid, as Emilio constructs his snazzy racing car? Do you hear excitement and joy in the children's inquisitive voices? Do you recognize the sound of eager participatory learners—laughter and delight? Do you hear children helping and encouraging one another? Do you hear the cooperating teacher continually modeling problem-solving techniques?

Look First and Foremost at the Walls

Are the walls covered with individualized artwork of the children? Is the artist's name scrawled in large wobbly letters here, there, and

Figure 3–3

anywhere on the paper? Are the colors in the paintings fresh and vivacious? Is there mixing and blending into other than primary colors by an aspiring Chagall? Are the paintings done on large (18-by-24-inch) white paper with wide bristle brushes? Are the children chatting as they paint alongside one another, rather than working on either side of a double easel, which makes conversation difficult to hold? Are there paper and material collages, finger paintings, and all manner of artistic expression on display?

Artwork can reveal a great deal about what a particular teacher feels is important in the life of a young child. The artwork can tell you if these young children have the freedom to express their feelings in artistic ways. Easels with fresh paper and paint need to be available at all times. They are as basic to the quality of children's young lives as the food they eat and the water they drink. Art helps young people interpret their world, tell their story in their very own way. Art affords children a special avenue for expressing themselves and working out unresolved issues. Art also gives children an opportunity to take risks,

Figure 3–4

to experiment with different media—paint, clay, collage, and papier-mâché—in an open-ended way. Here repetition is not frowned upon, but conversely considered an integral part of the learning process. The quality and uniqueness of the artwork, or lack of it, can offer you insight into the manner in which educational opportunities are provided here.

Look for Room Arrangement as Climate Control

Look next at tables and chairs (and desks) to see what their arrangement says to the children who live in that space. Look to see if there is a comfortable couch, covered in a soft floral print, where a teacher

Figure 3–5

can sit and read *Whistle for Willie* with three or four children snuggled close by. Look for library areas, or corners of comfort, that have large overstuffed pillows lining the wall and a plush carpet remnant covering the floor. Look for lofts, where two children can seclude themselves to work together on an alphabet puzzle board or the Great Gears Building Set. Look for carpeted graduated steps, where children can sit for an open discussion with their teacher, ensuring that everyone can be seen and heard. Look for the presence of a water or sand table or a woodworking bench that is being used. Look for pieces of furniture that are versatile and can double as a puppet theater or a grocery store. Look to see if there is an inviting child-sized table and chairs set for dinner in the pretend area. Is the table covered with a brightly colored cloth and graced with a pot of red

What to Listen and Look for in the Learning Environment • 35

geraniums? Having many tables and chairs to accommodate up to six children at each promotes an easy exchange of ideas and invites conversation among peers.

Several years ago I was consulting in a K–1 public school in Tappan, New York. It was lunchtime, which in many schools is usually a wild, loud time with hoards of children at long rectangular tables and teachers roaming the room, trying to maintain some sense of order. Here in Tappan, the lunchroom was filled with twenty small round tables that sat six children each. It was civilized, peaceful, and very homey. For me, this was a memorable occasion, seeing children so relaxed, enjoying both their meals and their tablemates. The furniture was an extension of an idea: that meals should be a pleasurable time for all concerned. The climate provided a quiet message about thoughtfulness, respect, appropriateness, and good decision making from the principal of the school.

Perhaps you have seen a three-year-old classroom where each chair had a child's name boldly printed on a piece of oak tag taped to its backrest. In that classroom a child had no choice in where to sit. It was always at the same table and next to the same two people. How does this make Benjamin feel when he really wants to sit next to his new buddy, Jaktar, and he knows it is not allowed? By chance, in your travels, you may have seen a large round table painted a heavenly shade of violet that sat just eighteen inches off the floor. Such a table, used for artwork, allows children and teacher to sit on the floor without a hint of the restriction that chairs provide. Comfortable couches and overstuffed chairs can create an atmosphere of intimacy and caring. Many young children like to be physically close to their adored teacher as they hear their favorite book read over and over again. Welcome the sight of Pooh Bear, Raggedy Ann, Raggedy Andy, or other stuffed animals or dolls in the book corner. Max knows that he can go there to be alone, to read a story to Pooh Bear, or to have a teacher read him *Mister Rabbit and the Lovely Present* for the third time that week.

At the early childhood centers of Reggio Emilia, Italy, one important part of their philosophy is the versatility of space and mobility of equipment. They move painted red wooden tables and chairs outdoors for lunchtime. They take easels outside to catch the early morning light. Latticework screens create special niches in the piazza, an open courtyard, where small groups of children or parents come

Figure 3–6

together for work or reflection. The planning of each day and the movement of furniture reflect a flexibility of spirit, a willingness to capture the beauty of the moment.

Active Activity Areas

If you were a classroom teacher, you may remember starting the morning with a group time. You may have considered this the most meaningful time that the group had together—even better than snack! This was a time for coming together to discuss what was happening in your world. You talked about real things that occurred on the playground, how Juan felt when Tony kicked his sand castle down and said it was dumb-looking. You talked about Claire's Bernese mountain dog, who suddenly became very ill on Thursday and died the next morning at the veterinary hospital. She told everyone how much she cried and how really upset and sad she was. Kylie announced that her cat ran away, and they never found him. You spoke about things that mattered and concerned all of you. There

Figure 3–7

were questions that needed answering or problems that needed to be solved. You also spoke about what was here and now, how Mario and Laura and every single person wanted to start his or her day. Each child, being allowed to follow her wishes, went to the activity area of her choice. Maybe Lawrence had been thinking about the pirate ship he was going to build with blocks while he was eating his cinnamon bagel and cream cheese for breakfast. Maybe Melissa had been daydreaming that very morning about putting on the pink tulle skirt and being a beautiful ballerina. Because you honored the way children think and feel, you set no limits for the number of children allowed in each area. Do you remember from your teaching career when ten children were in the block area at one time? It worked because the children made it work. And, if tempers became short, you asked the children to stop their work, come together as a group and figure out what to do next.

Can you imagine going into your own home and finding the living room, the dining room, or the kitchen closed for the day? The thought is almost unimaginable, yet I think about it each time I walk into an early childhood center and see the shelves of the pretend area or the block area turned around and their blank backs exposed to the children. I think about it, too, when the water table is drained and covered, or there is no paint or paper set up at the easels. Above all, all centers must be open each day so that children can have the opportunity to try the things they love to do most—to have the freedom to choose from the full array of activities.

Having activity areas within an early childhood room helps young people organize their world. The blocks are in the block area, the books and records are in the library, the dress-up clothes are in the pretend area. It all makes visual and cognitive sense. Young children feel comfortable knowing where to go to play and knowing, in part, what is expected of them.

Think about the following when you are in a classroom:

- Look for the degree of involvement in play. How interested are the children in their work?
- Look and listen for the children's conversation. Are the children the directors of their own repertory theater, or are the activities mainly teacher directed?
- How extensive are the props in each area? Do you see pads of paper and a juice can filled with sharpened pencils, so "Mom" or "Dad" can make out the morning shopping list? Are there five-by-seven-inch index cards with each child's name and telephone number in a stack by the telephone? That way Huiping can pretend to call home to tell her little brother what she has been doing at the center this morning. Are there rectangles of oak tag, red and purple magic markers, and construction tape all in baskets in the block corner? Then the young architects can make signs for their buildings.
- Is there a basket with three different kinds of lettuce and a cherry tomato by the guinea pig cage, so that Nathaniel and Toby can decide what treat Marmalade likes best?
- Do you hear Peggy say, "I'll help you set the table," while she is working in the pretend area? What does this tell you about the level of cooperative play?
- Do the children seem to be negotiating with one another and working through their own differences?
- Are there twenty activities going on simultaneously?
- Is the lively chatter of busy children a symphony of music to your ears?

The Movement of Children

You have listened to the sounds of the room, you have examined the four walls, and you have scrutinized the various activity areas on an individual basis. Now, it is time to sit back and look at the larger picture: the movement of children within their given space. Certain activities are, by their very nature, noisier than others. When a group of children are working together, they are figuring out things out loud, exchanging ideas, and reacting to what has just been said. That is the way it is supposed to be. These are the underpinnings of inquiry and knowledge. These are the sounds of learning.

"Make Glad the Heart of Childhood" (Church 1897)

A child needs a place to build a farm or a high-rise apartment and examine the shell of a horseshoe crab and the makings of a Baltimore oriole's nest. He needs a place to do a puzzle of a dentist or a sailboat and whip up a batch of chocolate chip cookies, bake them, and immediately have the time and place to sit down to eat them. A child needs a place to do his own artwork, mix red and blue paint, and watch a miracle happen. He needs a place to walk a balance beam, a place to run, jump, dance, and sing. He needs a place to tuck the baby doll safely in his crib and sing him his favorite lullaby. A child needs a place to be with his group and have space enough to sit comfortably, like a small island on a placid lake, and see all the pictures of *Owl Moon* without Joey's head being in the way. A child needs a place to go when his world falls apart where he can sit on his teacher's lap and cry if he feels like crying, or be alone, if that is what he wants to do most. A child's schoolroom needs to have many things—most of all a caring teacher who understands how deeply feeling and complex a child can be.

As you know, play areas serve an effective purpose in organizing a child's world. However, within that organized model, there should be great flexibility. If Adam, who is designing an extraterrestrial space station, is not allowed to use the Cuisenaire Rods to decorate his structure, then something important has been lost. Similarly, if Jeanne is dressed to the nines, sporting a gold lamé gown and dripping in jewels, she needs to be seen in all four corners of the room, and not be confined just to the pretend area. You may have been in centers where children are not allowed to leave the play area of their choice for a specific time period, and furthermore must leave the area after fifteen minutes, even if they are deeply involved in play. Certainly the teachers who set up this system did so for several reasons: They want to treat everyone fairly, giving each child equal time in each area. They also want to keep the children occupied and under control. The losses with this system can be immeasurable, however. Consider the frustration that Annie feels when, in the midst of her finger painting, she is asked to go to the library area, despite her yearning to finish her masterpiece. Perhaps the flow of traffic is more manageable with the system described, but the feeling of pride in a job well done cannot be realized. The movement of children within a given space is more than what meets the eye; it should be considered in a deeper sense. Young children should be allowed to grow through their work. They should be given ample time to complete their plans and accomplish their goals. Children's learning should not be short-circuited at the altar of a rigid classroom schedule.

Each classroom has its own set of routines, its own way of defining and creating its singular vigorous environment. For many early childhood programs, the morning meeting is the vehicle that begins the day for young children. This time can often be a high point, because, by its very nature, it exemplifies and clarifies what is yet to come. Young children like to know what the plan is, what is offered and what is allowable. This is the time when a teacher can bring to the children's attention that marble painting is ready and waiting for the young artists, that new street signs have been added to the block corner, and that potatoes, onions, eggs, salt, baking powder, and oil are waiting on a table for the young scientists to make potato pancakes. This is the time when children can choose how they want to start their day, in what area they want to play. It is also at this time that children come together to talk with their teacher and their peers about things that matter most to them. This is the time to ask questions about why Clarise was so mean, and called Antonia a little baby, and also to talk about why Sam's dad didn't have time to read him a story this morning when he came to school. If we give larger blocks of time to things that are meaningful to children, rather than to the rote learning of the calendar and the weather chart, then we open up the possibility of greater growth and satisfaction that come from having the time to work through a project. A teacher's thoughtful consideration and good judgment are necessary to determine how best to spend time in the classroom. It comes with knowing the interests of the children and following their lead.

Go for Good Design

There are logical thoughts to be considered when planning the design of a room. More-active activities are often placed side by side. Quieter activities are far distant from the blocks and the pretend area. Art activities should be close to the sink. These are givens. You may find it more inviting, particularly with very young children, to have the quieter activities near where the children enter the room. That way, Mom, Dad, or a grandparent can sit down with Caroline and read her a story or work alongside her with some pink play dough. Each room is so different, and the configuration of the room decides a great deal in advance for us. Teachers work around what they have, hoping to create the best possible learning environment. You may have seen a classroom with too much open space, which encouraged running with wild abandon. The arrangement, or lack of thoughtful arrangement, can have an impact on an entire program. Room arrangement is serious business. Each classroom must be judiciously and carefully planned, but we must always be mindful that changes can be part of the plan.

The Drama of It All

Children are natural dramatists. The world is their theater. The house lights have always just been dimmed, and the curtain is permanently up. The script is constantly in the process of being written, the roles are interchangeable, the cast of characters varies with the moment—and the show goes on. Teachers can also be part of children's play. They need to be fully cognizant that they are neither the director nor the producer, but rather just members of the cast. Young children need to feel ownership of the script.

A teacher can play an influential part in subtle ways. She sets the stage, using her good judgment with room design and artfully choosing all the various props for the room. A teacher needs to be keenly aware of what is age appropriate for her group, always keeping in mind the range of abilities within a given class. In setting up a classroom at the beginning of the year, a teacher can, if possible, make sure that children have familiar puzzles that they have mastered from the year before. This, along with open-ended manipulatives, such as wooden beads and Legos, can give them a sense of both comfort and competency, which will allow them to move ahead. A wise teacher will become immediately aware of materials that are too difficult for the moment. A wise teacher will have many things available, but not necessarily on display. The contents of the room should be categorized, well labeled, and within easy reach so they're readily available when just the right time to introduce them comes along. Classrooms need to be simple in the beginning and become more complex as the term progresses.

Praise for Project Work

Project work is engaging for many reasons. Ideas, coming from the conversations of children, provide inspiration for teachers and children to gather and work on material together. The work is far-ranging, not only for its intellectual and artistic challenges but also for the audience that it reaches. Parents can become an integral part of the plan, as both active partners and participants. They can help design and build a table with grow lights to start the garden seedlings indoors or join the children on a field trip. Parents are also eager readers of documentation that the teachers have recorded and displayed within the room. It gives parents a window into their children's lives at school. They read about conversations and discussions that have taken place. They see drawings that the children have done and photographs of their children as they work. Documentation follows the children and their work from the incipient ideas through all the highways and byways to their final destination. Through this instrument, children, teachers, and parents can revisit and rejoice in the learning process over and over again (Cadwell 1997).

The more project work that the children and teachers take on together, the greater the participation and, hence, the depth of learning will be. Project work brings teachers and children together to plan each step of the way as they create their own curriculum. Project work builds a community where children and teachers are linked together through their interests and joint endeavors. With project work, children have many opportunities to work cooperatively and to problem solve. Each has a responsibility to him- or herself and to each member of the group. It is teaching at its best . . . learning from one another (Helm and Katz 2001).

Completing the Circle

As each day could begin by coming together as a group, so could each day end. It is all about listening and sharing the highlights and dark moments of the day. It is a powerful way to support one another, to feel proud of one's own growth, the growth of a fellow student, and the accomplishments of the group. Beginning and ending each day in this way moves young children forward toward realizing their own potential and acknowledging a sense of community building.

Summary

When you are in a classroom, you have the opportunity to do many things: to feel the climate that permeates the space; to listen and look for indicators that children are actively involved in the learning process; to see if the cooperating teacher is interacting with the children in a positive way. You have time to reflect: Are there many occasions for individual, small-group, and large-group activities? Are there blocks of time set aside for group discussion? Do children move freely from one activity area to another, doing so according to their own clock? You have time to observe: Are all activity centers always open so that children can practice becoming decision makers? How does the teacher arrange the room with all the tools of learning? How do children and the teacher work together to deepen their understanding of the world? These are the ways you listen and look at the learning environment, so that you, in turn, can have that same expectation for your student.

Reflective Questions

1. Are there additional sounds and sights in the classroom to which you will pay attention?

2. Do you regard yourself more as a guest than a facilitator of change when you are in the classroom? Why?

3. What is your moral obligation if you see a course of action that *isn't* happening in the classroom? Will you pose a question, say something about it, or just stay silent?

4. How would you describe the energy level of the children? What does this say to you?

5. If you feel strongly that room arrangement affects the way that children learn, will you sketch and share a new floor plan with the cooperating teacher and your student?

6. What activities does the class offer that allow children to make choices for themselves?

Facilitating Student Learning

After reading this chapter, you should understand

- what guidelines you will set up for your student's first day at the field placement site;
- the type of work in which a student teacher will initially be engaged;
- what you should expect the student to look for in the classroom;
- that it is the student's responsibility to ask for ample discussion time with the cooperating teacher;
- how important it is for the student to engage in ongoing self-evaluation;
- how the reflective journal enhances the learning process for the student, the cooperating teacher, and the supervisor;
- that supervisors can have their own style for responding to reflective journals;
- how important it is for each student to *write* his own personal credo; and
- how the student can be both a giver and a receiver of gifts.

The early childhood college student and his respective college have mutual obligations to one another. The student should strive to do the best possible job in his field placement. The college should strive to select the best possible teacher with whom the student will be working. In the beginning of the field placement, it is important that the student, Miku, has time just to be there, to absorb the atmosphere around him, to observe the layout of the room and the use of materials. He will want to study the relationships among the children. He will be observing how the cooperating teacher thinks, acts, and responds to various situations. What is the quality of her interactions with her staff? How responsive are the children to her? If possible, ask the student to arrange a meeting with the cooperating teacher before the first day on the job. Miku could put together a list of prepared questions. He should ask what his responsibilities will be, so that he will be very clear about this. Remind him to tell the cooperating teacher about any assignments that he has from the college. Ask that he share his syllabus with her or make a photocopy for her. Suggest that he get a list of the names of all the children in the class.

Guidelines for the Student's First Day

You could distribute the following guidelines to your students at the beginning of the term:

- Ask the cooperating teacher how she would like to be addressed.
- Inquire about and follow your center's dress code.
- Arrive well before the children are scheduled to arrive.
- Make it known to the cooperating teacher that you are willing to do whatever needs to be done within the classroom—and you would welcome her direction.
- Remember that the cooperating teacher is looking forward to working with you and having you in her class.
- Give the cooperating teacher an index card with your name, address, telephone number, email address, fax number if available, and a schedule of the times you will be in her class.

Mentoring Early Childhood Educators

- Give the cooperating teacher the name and phone number of your supervisor, after you have sought permission, and the dates and times of her visits.
- Take copious notes about all that you see and do in class. Be specific and detailed about your observations.
- Set your goals down on paper.
- Don't be afraid to ask questions.
- Be yourself.

Taking the First Steps

If this is the first time the student will be in a leadership role in the classroom, there is a lot to think about. As a student teacher, Miku may feel anxious and not quite sure what his role is. He may be worried about whether the children will like him or not. This is all perfectly natural. Fortunately, young children are, for the most part, open, accepting, and affectionate. Many of the uncertainties will quickly fade into the background. Miku should take his cues from the cooperating teacher and look to her for guidance. At group time he should learn to sit between Eartha and Jane if he sees that they continue to chat and are having difficulty settling down. He should continually scan the room to look for trouble spots.

Starting Small

In the beginning of the field placement, the focus will be on working with individual children or small groups—wherever the cooperating teacher feels the student is needed most. Chances are he may start out at a table with three or four children playing Candy Land or the Very Hungry Caterpillar game. That way Miku will have the opportunity to get to know a small group of children by name and help them with or join in the game. Working with a small group allows him to focus more easily and to see, firsthand, how accepting young children can be. Later on, after more work with children, he will want to interact with larger numbers of children at one time. He may try reading a story to eight or ten children. This allows him to see what the inherent problems are in maintaining attention and answering questions without losing the story line. Just finding a space that has ample room for everyone's comfort may be one of the initial challenges.

Things to Think About

There are so many things to think about in whatever the student sets out to do. Working with young children may spark "the wheels of the bus" to go at an accelerated pace. Children move quickly, and oftentimes their attention span has a limited time frame. Miku may reconsider his footwear, seeing the need to be in the block area in record-breaking time, since tempers can flare in split seconds. Being there in time makes all the difference. The student will find himself thinking in more depth about what he says and when he says it. Miku will be choosing his words with much greater care. Young children have tender feelings that are easily hurt. They may also have their own agendas. For example, they may be missing Mommy or Daddy, or perhaps they don't feel just right in the tummy. Their needs may require tending before Miku can read a story or start cleanup time.

Gaining a New Perspective

The student will get to know the children's voices and recognize in an instant when play is not going in the right direction. Miku will learn how to read each child's body language, knowing what it means if Marcia is standing still with her eyes cast down. He will get to know what combinations of children work well together and which need to be more carefully watched. He will be aware that Awni can be counted on to be a mediator and that Rose is the take-charge person in the pretend area. He will figure out which children are steady and more dependable. He will recognize which children are more volatile and need to be kept in his line of vision. He will also know, as time goes by, how important it is to be able to see what everyone is doing at any given moment. This ties in directly to effective room arrangement. Hopefully, as his knowledge and experience base builds, Miku will become a good anticipator. The ability to anticipate situations is an invaluable tool.

Organizing All of It

Question if your student has noticed how important it is to have the room, as well as its contents, well organized. Did he see what a difference it made when Ismail wanted to use the magnetic design board and he knew exactly where it was kept? Does he recognize how essential it is to think in an organized fashion about everything that he undertakes? Does Miku understand that not only are the cooperating teacher and her assistants role models for Eartha, Jane, Awni, and Ismail, but he is a role model too?

Talk, Talk, Talk

Part of the student's job in the field placement experience is arranging to have enough time to talk with the cooperating teacher. These are critical conversations. Miku needs time to have his questions answered. They need time together to think through various issues that have come up in the classroom. He needs time to plan ahead. This can be complicated, because both of them have enormously busy schedules with prior commitments. But having this time together is a vital link in making the program successful. If this presents difficulties, then it is appropriate for you to work with the student and cooperating teacher to construct an alternative plan.

The student can also bring questions back to his university classroom. Let the professor and Miku's fellow students brainstorm specific issues together. If Rose, the take-charge young lady in the pretend area, always remains the one to direct the play, how does this impact

Hendrik and Camille, who are not so self-assured? Should this drama be allowed to continue? This type of discussion with his peers may help expand your student's thoughts and strategies.

One of the things you may find yourself thinking about is discussing interpersonal relationships with your student. How would he go about trying to implement change in order to give each child more space in which to grow? From your perspective, from what you have observed, both Hendrik and Camille need to know what their rights are in the pretend area. They need to understand that they should be allowed to speak up on their own behalf and to play the roles that they are longing to play. This could mean that Miku needs to be in close proximity to where the action is taking place. Sometimes a well-timed question could start a child to rethink his or her options. Miku could ask Hendrik and Camille, "How do you feel about being the engineers of the train, rather than always being passengers? It is important to tell Rose that you need a turn to be in charge." Of course, the scenario needs to be repeated many times so that children are able to internalize the idea that they can be more in control of themselves. They also need to be reminded of their successes often. For some children this is difficult to do, as building self-confidence is a gradual process. Trying to foster behaviors that allow a youngster to feel strong and confident is a good part of what early childhood educators do. These early years can be looked on as the opportune time to work toward self-actualization before unsuitable patterns of behavior become too firmly set.

There is another issue that you and your student may want to examine. Does Miku come to his own determination about how to regard each child? Does he realize that the cooperating teacher may have certain biases that could color his view of who Claudia and George are? Will you urge Miku to trust himself and rely on his own good judgment?

Self-Evaluation for the Student

The following list can serve as an invaluable tool, not only for the student but also for the cooperating teacher and the supervisor. These questions can be used as a basis for a two- or three-way discussion, or they can be answered in written form—your choice. These questions ask the student to take a critical view of himself, to become deeply reflective about his work. This is an important professional responsibility for the student, which can be done at both the beginning and the end of the semester.

- How involved are you with the children? What kinds of things are you sharing with them about yourself?
- When working with an individual child, how do you stay connected with what the rest of the group is doing?
- With which types of children do you feel less patient? What are you doing to overcome this bias?
- What is the quality of interaction that you have with the cooperating teacher and the other adults in the room? What could you do to improve this?
- What pertinent questions have you asked the cooperating teacher? What questions do you still need to ask?
- What type of input do you have in helping to plan the curriculum with the cooperating teacher? How could you expand this, if this is an option?
- How much initiative do you demonstrate in introducing either spontaneous or planned small-group activities?
- What do you see as your strengths in presenting yourself as a professional? What are you presently working to improve?
- What kind of situations propel you to go the extra mile? Describe.
- What kind of situations do you shy away from? Why? How will you try to remedy this?
- How effectively have you correlated your course work with your field placement assignment?
- How often do you have the opportunity to interact with parents? What is the quality of these interactions?
- What issues have come up in this placement that have challenged your thinking the most?
- What practices in this placement are you most comfortable with?
- What have been your goals for your field placement experience? What have you succeeded in accomplishing? What remains to be done?

- How has your supervisor been a resource person for you? Has she provided you with articles, books, ideas, and topics for discussion? How has she been a wellspring of encouragement and support?

The Reflective Journal

During the course of the semester, your student will be asked to keep a reflective journal. This journal will be an important source of information for the cooperating teacher, the supervisor, and the classroom professor. The emphasis of the writing is not merely listing the student's observations, but rather recording a thoughtful analysis of what the student has internalized about his work. The student has ten journal questions to answer that span a fifteen-week semester. Often the fieldwork experience does not start until several weeks into the semester. The list of topics is given to the student at the beginning of the term. As the supervisor, you have different options. Perhaps you will want to read the reflective journal responses while you are visiting the student. In that way, you can comment upon Miku's work immediately and jot down questions or phrases to remind you of what you want to discuss further with him. Another option is to take the journal responses home with you, read them at your leisure, and mail your written responses back to the student. Much is dependent upon the time you have available and what your expectations are. Hopefully, the cooperating teacher will have read the responses and made her comments as well. For ease in handling, request that the journal responses be written in a three-ring notebook, so pages can be easily removed. Thus, from the very beginning, a four-way process of communication is firmly established. Sample guiding questions are listed on pages 56–57. Following the reflective journal questions are examples of responses, from both students and supervisors. The examples of responses from supervisors reflect the two different approaches: (1) the immediate response, written right in the journal at the time of the visit and (2) the written response, which is done following the visit and mailed to the student.

Each student receives the following statement in addition to the reflective journal questions:

Dear Student,

One of the important attributes a teacher can possess is the ability to be a reflective practitioner. Learning is a process by which each person constructs meaning from his or her experience. We build knowledge by observing, documenting, reflecting, and questioning. The intent of this journal is to provide you with a vehicle for thinking. It is not enough to just report on what you see or do in a classroom. Reflection requires that you think about what has occurred. Ask yourself: What if . . . ? What worked? What didn't work? What might I do differently? and What are the possibilities here? As professionals, we are potential researchers into the nature of teaching in our classrooms.

The Reflective Journal
Your reflective journal will help you think about your reading, consider what is occurring in your field placement, and remember what you have learned from both. Each week you are expected to respond to one of the questions listed below.

The journal will provide an opportunity for an ongoing dialogue between you, your cooperating teacher, your supervisor, and myself. The intent of the four-way journal writing is to offer us the opportunity to make meanings through our observations and questions about curriculum. Each of us is a learner and explorer in this process; each point of view deepens our understandings and offers multiple ways of seeing.

The three or four-way journal offers each of us an opportunity to share stories, raise questions, and respond to each other. They are a place for figuring out the complexities of teaching and curriculum. If your cooperating teacher is unable to participate in this process, please let me know immediately and I will help you find another placement.

It is your responsibility to give your cooperating teacher and your supervisor your journal for review and written comment in a timely manner. All responses must be word-processed using 12-point Times New Roman, double spaced. Journals are submitted to the field supervisor in a folder with pockets every three weeks. All entries must be numbered, titled, and dated. At the end of the semester you will have completed ten entries. Each is worth ten points and the journal is seventy percent of your final grade. Late work will not be accepted.

Guiding Questions

Journal One

After reading the first chapter in *The Creative Curriculum* and Peter Haiman's article "Developing a Sense of Wonder in Young Children," think about your classroom. What is in the room and how is the room arranged? How are materials displayed and made available? How does this environment encourage a sense of wonder?

Journals Two and Three

Observe the children as they work together with different materials and as they interact with one another and with adults. What are they wondering about? What arouses their curiosity? What questions are they asking (though not always verbally)? Think about other ways they make their questions known. (Two separate entries.)

Journal Four

What have you learned, so far, about how your cooperating teacher plans the curriculum? How are children's experiences and understandings documented?

Journal Five

After reading Ann Martin's article "Social Studies in Kindergarten: A Case Study," think about how issues of social justice and fairness are addressed in your classroom. Have you seen occasions that offered opportunities for curriculum that addresses such issues?

Journal Six

Observe a child/children working with blocks. Describe what you see and hear. What are you learning about the child/children through their block play? Further, what are you coming to understand about what children gain by working with blocks?

Journal Seven

What do you notice when children are involved in dramatic play (in the dramatic play area, outdoors, and so on)? What do they talk about? What ideas come up for them?

Journal Eight

Record a child's story or the retelling of a book or a child's description of his or her work. How do the child's words help you understand the child?

Journal Nine

1. What materials are provided and how are children using them?

2. How do you respond to children's work? What do you say? What do you think the children are learning from your reaction to their work?

Journal Ten

This is your final entry. What important ideas have you come away with from this course? What has been most helpful to you? What did you struggle with? What suggestions might you offer us?

The journal statements, assignments, and guiding questions were written by Professor Sheila Hanna, Chair of Early Childhood Curriculum, Westchester Community College, Valhalla, New York.

A Student's Response to Journal One

Journal One: After reading the first chapter in *The Creative Curriculum* and Peter Haiman's article *Developing a Sense of Wonder in Young Children*, think about your classroom. What is in the room and how is the room arranged? How are materials displayed and made available? How does this environment encourage a sense of wonder?

In reflecting on Diane Trister Dodge's messages in the environment, compared to my field classroom, I have become aware of some messages which are not reflected in my room, although many are reflected in varying degrees.

In my field classroom, for example, the message "this is a good place to be" is partially conveyed. Although the walls are of a neutral color, furniture is clean, and children's artwork is displayed at eye level, there is very little bright color usage to attract interest to selective areas, nor are there colorful plants, pillows, or tablecloths. Artwork display is also "cluttered" looking.

The message "you belong here" is also partially clear due to severe space limitations. There are no cubbies in the room for personal belongings—only a row of hooks on one wall which is too high for the children to reach. Their blankets are stored loose, on top of the stacked cots, and their extra clothes are in individual plastic bags in a storage bin. On the positive side, "you belong here" is revealed via child-sized furniture, a variety of books which reflect people of different ethnic backgrounds and abilities, as well as dolls which are reflective of the children's ethnic heritage.

The message "you can do many things on your own and be independent" is also only partially apparent in this classroom setting. Although tabletop toys are always available, labeled and within reach, art supplies are not accessible to children at all times. Instead, only specific media are made available for use at certain times/days and are "teacher" selected and supervised. Paper, crayons, and markers are neatly stored and within reach for the children to use at any time they choose during free play. Many of the toys are also labeled in Spanish (which constitutes more than one-half of our class population), allowing teachers who don't speak Spanish to learn and use words in the child's native tongue.

There is no job chart illustrating children's responsibilities, although there is a "helper chart" used during morning meeting, allowing children to see who will be the helpers for the day. They can also see whose turn is coming up soon and anticipate for the next day.

The outdoor play structure is slightly too large for a few of the smaller three-year-olds, but most manage fairly well; and there is plenty of outdoor space for them to run around, which encourages their gross motor skill development. Our playground time slot, however, is far too limited, lasting only about fifteen minutes immediately following lunch. Sadly, I feel this relays a poor message to the children about the importance of outdoor play and physical activity. Shared space is the problem in this school, and pre-K gets kicked off the playground when the older children come out at their scheduled time. I have expressed my concern about this situation, and alternate time slots are being investigated to allow our classroom more time outdoors.

The message "you can get away and be by yourself when you need to" is not a message that I see conveyed in this classroom setting. Although there are two large beanbag chairs near the book rack, as well as a tape player and headphones for "books on tape" stories, the area is not really a quiet area, nor is it clearly separated from the rest of the room.

Other than anticipation by the children when new toys, books, or puzzles are introduced, I'm sorry to say that I do not feel this classroom encourages a sense of wonder. I am confident, however, that it will by the time I complete this course.

A Supervisor's Response

The following is one example of a response written by a supervisor at the time of the site visit.

> Jennifer, I try not to fancy myself a psychologist when I hear a child's story. What is important about these emotional possibilities is that we be aware the stories *may* present clues to a child's concerns. The other suggestion is to keep copies of children's stories so that we may, after filing a few, have more documentation of emotions. If these are blatant, constant concerns, it may be important to share them with a counselor. To me the major value exists in providing kids with opportunities to create stories—to grow in language skills—to accompany drawings and, as you say, to rework stories they've heard into their own creations.

Good, good luck—I wish you the best. Keep going in our field, we are lucky to have you, and so are the children.

Jo

A Student's Response to Journal Eight

Journal Eight: Record a child's story or the retelling of a book or a child's description of his or her work. How do the child's words help you understand the child?

Storytelling in our classroom is a daily activity. Sometimes one story per day, sometimes two or three. Occasionally, we will have a story during morning meeting, but always, there is a story after lunch, right before quiet time. Also, occasionally, we may have another short story after snack, if there is time before dismissal, but this is rare. We also have a library period once a week on Monday morning, where the children are read a story, then each one selects his/her own book to take back to class for the week.

Following is Dylan's story, November 12:

Once upon a time, there was a big round rock. A person saw the rock and the rock sat still. It did not do nothing and the boy waited and waited and waited and waited and waited until he got an angry face and then he sat on the rock. He punched the rock and kicked it, and nothing happened. Then the boy turned into a lion. Since he was very angry, he turned into a lion and his hair was changing into all different colors—black, orange and brown and red and blue.

And then there was letters in front of his eyes. Then he felt happy and turned back into a person. Then he found a girl and the girl helped him drive the car and do all the stuff he needed to do. Then he saw a rainbow and he was happy. Then he got angry again. The End.

Two items should be noted regarding this child's story. First, earlier that morning the book *Sylvester and the Magic Pebble* by William Steig was read to him, which has the main character (Sylvester, a donkey) turning into a big rock when he is face-to-face with a hungry lion. Second, the child was drawing pictures as he was telling the story.

From Dylan's story I have learned two things: One, that children impose upon themselves fictional attributes which they have heard in stories. Although at four years of age Dylan has really a good sense of reality and fantasy, he interrelates fantasy into his reality. Second is that children reveal their own fears and frustrations through their personal stories. Knowing Dylan, the child, and understanding the difficult home life he has, brings his reality (anger and fear) to light in his story. He was having a rough day, and was quite angry himself on this day, which is revealed through his story.

A Supervisor's Response

The following is an example of a response written by the supervisor following the visit and mailed to the student.

Romaine,

The excellence of your work shines throughout this reflective journal. I applaud your keen powers of observation and your thoughtful analysis of the classroom where you are doing your field placement. Being able to recognize both the positive and the negative aspects of this particular environment has allowed you to crystallize your thoughts about what remains to be done to make it a "better" place for children. However, let me add a cautionary note about how to present "criticism" in a reflection of a given situation. I say this, even though we both fully understand that all your suggestions are put forth with the best intentions for improving the learning climate. Let me urge you to turn around the *form* of your observations to put them into questions. Criticism is more easily accepted if it is well cushioned and less direct. For example, you speak about the environment, saying: "there is very little bright color usage to attract interest to selective areas." Instead, could you pose the question, "In what areas could we think of adding brightly colored items in order to attract the children's interest?" This is also opening up an avenue for action. You have also mentioned, "The message 'you can get away and be by yourself when you need to' is not a message that I see conveyed in this setting. Although there are two large beanbag chairs near the book rack, . . . the area is not really a quiet area, nor is it clearly separated from the rest of the room." This could be turned around and stated in softer terms: "Considering the fact that we have two beanbag chairs, a book rack, and a tape player, how could we section off this area of the room in order to create a quiet area for the children?"

You mentioned the limited use of bright colors, which make a room look more lively and attractive. Is it possible to mount the children's paintings on large pieces of oak tag, which could act as frames for their artwork? Could you also, for example, use colorful magazine pictures, of men and women on construction jobs, bridges, skyscrapers, country scenes, and so on, mounted on colored paper or oak tag for the block area? In order to enliven the library corner, would you consider to first laminate and then post the dust jackets of half a dozen picture books that you have in the room?

Can you speak to your cooperating teacher about the value of having plants in your room? Plants can serve many purposes; they lift our spirits as well as afford children the opportunity to take care of living things. Plants exemplify the cycle of life, birth, growth, and death. Having seedlings or plants as part of a classroom enables children to become acquainted with part of the natural world. They can learn how each of us can help to nourish a part of the environment. Personally, I feel very strongly about the importance of introducing this concept to very young children.

If the artwork display is cluttered-looking, could you and the cooperating teacher think through your system of sending artwork home on a more regular basis? The display of artwork is greatly enhanced by simplicity. Leaving space around an object gives it greater prominence and delights the eye.

You have a difficult situation because of your limited space. However, it is terribly important that children feel that they have a place to call their own. Would the center allow hooks to be moved down to the child's level, so you could then attach photographs alongside them? Since cubbies are not available, would it be possible to have a shelf constructed above the hooks so that extra clothing could be stored in shoe boxes? The boxes could also be painted a bright color (by the child) and then have each child's name printed neatly on one end. Have you thought about the other possibility of having a sectioned-off shelf built at the floor level, so that each child's blanket could be stored there? All these things could help a child feel her own sense of place and foster independence.

As far as the message "You can do many things on your own and be independent," have you discussed with your cooperating teacher about the need for greater accessibility of art materials? Having a wide variety of art materials available each day helps children become good decision makers. This also gives them the opportunity to express themselves in creative and artistic ways. Could some of the supplies be placed in clear plastic bins, marked with a sample of what the contents are, and placed on low shelves within their reach? Paper, crayons, and markers, although staples of any early childhood program, have a limited range. Children need to be able to construct items that have various weights, textures, and colors—this expands their repertoire and also allows them to use their small muscles in different ways.

I must say that it "hurt" me to read about the short number of minutes that are allotted to three-year-olds for outdoor activity—and what an inappropriate time slot for them! Young children need to be able to move their bodies and explore the world. Wonderful that you are following up on the possibility of both extending the time and changing the assigned time that the children presently have.

I have touched briefly on the importance of having a place of one's own in the classroom. This is somehow compounded when I learn that there is really no separate place to be by oneself when the need arises. Will you and the cooperating teacher give priority to creating a space that speaks of comfort and beckons a needy child?

Romaine, knowing how invested you are in your work, I too feel confident that you will do your utmost to create a sense of wonder with this particular group.

Once again, it was a great pleasure to read your reflections. Your keen eye and fine sensibilities are present throughout your writing.

Carol

Additional journal responses by both students and supervisors can be found in Appendix B (page 99).

A Student's Commitment

As a supervisor your have looked long and hard at your student. You have looked to see whether he has made a commitment to the field of early childhood education. For the student, doing the best possible job he can is tightly bound to his own personal philosophy of education. Being a professional, or being on his way to becoming one, the student has been involved in a process of decision making and self-evaluation. Because education is a helping profession, he has already demonstrated his deep concern for others as well as his decision to spend time with children. What an excellent beginning!

Being an educator is exemplified by having a great love of learning and being an ongoing learner throughout a lifetime. It is this love of learning, of inquiry, that educators hope to impart to others. This is what propels you forward to navigate each day. Underlying these tenets is a fundamental truth that teachers find their greatest satisfactions in turning other human beings on to their own personal growth and fulfillment. Educators must have this firm commitment in place, for there will be days or particular groups of children that will call for unbelievable patience and forbearance. Educators can count on being tested in many ways on many days—that is part of the job. The supervisor looks for this commitment in each student.

A Supervisor's Assessment

As a supervisor you will want to be sensitive to many things. You will want to assess where your student is as he begins his field placement work. Then, you will want to look for changes as you observe his work. When you look at your student, you will want to think in terms of both what you see the student doing and what the student writes. There will be times when a student expresses a depth of feeling and understanding in his writing that is not as evident when you watch him working in the classroom. If you can, as the term progresses, try to determine the degree to which your student is seen as a team player. How much interaction takes place between the adults in the room? Do you sense that there is mutual respect for one another? Have you seen this increase over the term? You will want to look at your student's organizational skills. If Miku is setting up a small group project, has he thought it through in advance so that all the necessary equipment is on hand? If appropriate, has your student first tried the project on his own, to be sure if it is suitable for the age group with whom he is working? How responsive has your student been with the children? Is he forthcoming in his conversations, becoming less tentative and more self-assured in answering the children's questions? Do you recognize that he is more relaxed? Is he able to inject some humor into his thoughts, to lighten up and take himself less seriously? Does he respond good-naturedly when asked to carry out a task—and then do a thorough job? Is he constantly surveying the room, trying to judge where his efforts could best be used? Is Miku more open in conversation and contributing more to the three-way dialogue at your conferences?

Toward the end of the term, you may look at your student in a new light, acknowledging his growth within the classroom setting. You have watched him working with both adults and children. You have seen him explore new ideas and discard old views that did not work well. You have watched how his thinking has changed, how he has crystallized his thoughts. You have watched your student mature.

Thoughts on Writing a Personal Credo

You may want to ask your student to write his own personal credo. You may also want to share with him a copy of the following thoughts and ask him to comment on these beliefs:

> Be a believer in the goodness of children. Be present for them whenever you are with them. Be enthusiastic about your work, despite its sometimes trying or repetitive nature. Think about the safety of children—both physical and psychological—in whatever you do. Know how important it is *just* to engage in conversation with children. Know that being a supportive figure in the children's lives for the time that you are with them counts a lot.
>
> Also consider having the student reflect on and respond to the following statements:
>
> Give extra time if needed before the center opens or at home. Be willing to get your hands dirty. If paint gets splattered on your pants, just make the best of it. Remember that your tone of voice can convey a message in and of itself. Be aware that young children place great weight upon all the things you say and do. Know that it is a momentous and hilarious occasion for children

if a teacher drops a freshly made apple pie on the floor as she takes it out of the oven. Children need to know that even teachers make mistakes. Encourage the laughter of children by being playful and silly. Let your inner pleasure show itself through your facial expressions and body posture. Being a warm, sympathetic, and compassionate friend is giving a gift to children that they will always carry with them, tucked into a private corner of their mind.

The Student Can Be a Giver of Gifts

Having made it known, early on, that the student is willing to do whatever needs to be done, he must put his best foot forward and discuss his ideas with the cooperating teacher. Perhaps he is good with growing things and will bring in seed catalogs for spring planting. Perhaps he plays the guitar and would like to teach the future farmers to sing "Five Green and Spotted Frogs." Whatever his strengths may be, he should share them with his cooperating teacher so that his talents can be incorporated into the classroom. This is how he lets those around him know who he really is. By giving of himself, he is helping to build a community within those all-important four walls. There are many ways to give of oneself that can make a difference in the lives of children—and in the student's own life as well.

Gifts from the Other Side

There are, for the student teacher, great rewards that come from giving the best he has to offer. Seeing the look on Ella Mae's face when her marigold seed bursts through the earth counts for a lot. Watching her tenderly tend and talk to her plant tells the student that this youngster has been touched by a sense of wonder. There is also a look of trust that Eiko has as she puts her hand in his to walk back to the classroom after a tearful good-bye with Dad. There will be notes to cherish. There will be words, shy words of love from children: "I had a lovely time at nursery school, I hope I'll see you every day" or "I will miss you very much, I loved when you looked at my buildings." There will be notes from parents expressing thanks for helping their children learn to be excited about the accomplishments of others. There will be pictures drawn, pictures taken, and lovely thoughts made into books. There will be cupcakes made, decorated, baked, and eaten in celebration of birthdays or last days together. There can be letters, phone calls, child-made gifts, and visits to the student's home. There will be many hugs and kisses. There are all kinds of reminders of what connections can mean and what commitment can bring. These are the gifts that are long remembered.

Summary

The student will want to think about preparing himself for the first day of the field placement. He will be looking to the cooperating teacher for guidance in his initial work with individuals and small groups. He will want to be aware of the role that organization plays in classroom management. He will need to plan for ample time to meet and talk with the cooperating teacher. He will seek to interact with parents only after asking permission from the cooperating teacher. Miku will use his creative skills and talents with the group. He will work toward taking on more of the leadership role. Throughout his work he will evaluate his own strengths and weaknesses. He will be thinking in terms of making a personal commitment to the field of early childhood education. He will, after much reflection, write his own personal credo. He will be a giver of gifts and take great satisfaction in receiving gifts as well.

Reflective Questions

1. Of the guidelines given to students on their first day in the classroom, are there any that you would challenge? Why?

2. How will you urge your student to respond if the cooperating teacher can't seem to find the time to sit and talk with him?

3. Do you feel it advisable for the student to take over the leadership of the entire group at any point during the semester? If so, in what types of situations would you recommend he do so?

4. If you feel some of the reflective journal questions are too invasive, how would you change them?

5. Can you think of alternative ways for supervisors to respond to the reflective journal? Describe.

Mentoring Early Childhood Educators

Handling the Challenging Issues

Objectives

After reading this chapter, you should understand

- various methods of working with a resistant student teacher, teacher, cooperating teacher, or director;
- ways of accommodating the different learning styles of your students;
- some of the complications of counseling out a student from the program;
- how to help a student move on; and
- that challenges can be seen as opportunities.

Within any group of students, there will be those who have more natural ability and those who have less. There will be those who are enthusiastic learners and those who are lacking in motivation. There will be students who are open, cooperative, and inspire you with their creativity. And, occasionally, there will be the resistant student with whom it can be difficult to work.

Working with a Resistant Student

At some point you will experience or already have experienced working with a resistant student. It is not easy. There are no simple answers on how to resolve the issues. And, of course, each student is different and must be looked at carefully, with great sensitivity.

One of the approaches that you might consider in working with a resistant student is simply to try to understand the student better. What is it about the work that Kiri finds difficult? What is keeping her from putting her best foot forward? Try to ascertain if someone has said something to upset her. See if you can determine if she feels underappreciated or not allowed to do all she feels she is capable of doing. Perhaps it is something that you have said that she misinterpreted. There is also the possibility that there are pressing problems at home that are interfering with her ability to focus on her work. Whatever the reason may be, your empathy may be instrumental in getting to the crux of the problem.

It could be possible that the student is resentful of her placement and the lack of leadership from her cooperating teacher. Kiri may feel that she should be placed in a school that has higher standards. She may feel that her work at Central School is a waste of her time. In this case, there is much that needs to be discussed. Considering your own work schedule, could you set up several meetings, so that you could stay in close touch with one another? This could be done by telephone or email between site visits. Try to talk through the difficulties or frustrations that Kiri is feeling. Ask her to write down what is disturbing her each day. That way you have specific items to go over together. There are times when a negative experience, though difficult at the moment, can have a positive result. Ask Kiri to speak directly to the cooperating teacher to see if the two of them can work things out together. Then, if this meeting is not fruitful, suggest that all three of you meet together. This will be an opportunity to model appropriate ways of presenting ideas so that people are willing to listen to you. This may also be an opportunity for you to address specific areas that need to be clarified. As you talk, you may want to make a list of what you have discussed and leave this with the cooperating teacher. Then, if you have determined that, for many reasons,

Mentoring Early Childhood Educators

the placement is intolerable, you could consider reassigning the student to a different site.

As a supervisor you have your own expectations of what a student's performance should be. You should restate these standards and make them very clear. Strive to convey to Kiri that you are willing to look at the problem and work with her. However, the bottom line is that she must take the ultimate responsibility of helping herself and improving her performance in the classroom.

On occasion, you may come across a resistant cooperating teacher who declines to join the three-way dialogue. Unfortunately, the time that is available to conference with the student and the co-operating teacher is at noon, usually the cooperating teacher's lunch or prep time. So her decision not to join you may not always be a sign of resistance. Certainly you will want to invite her to join you on both your first and your second site visit. By then, she will have had the opportunity to read your written comments about the first observation and may rethink her former decision. When time allows, seek her opinion on how Kiri is doing. Ask what she sees as Kiri's greatest strengths and weaknesses. See if she has suggestions for what you might do to contribute to her base of knowledge. Make every effort to thank the cooperating teacher for all that she has done on the student's behalf. You can go only so far in asking her to give up her time to join you. If she sees it as an opportunity, then you will work together in a collaborative manner, which is both exciting and re-warding. If she chooses not to join you, you and your student must treat this decision with the greatest respect. This is *her* classroom and it is *her* choice. Documentation of what the college expects from the cooperating teacher is sent to the center or school in advance of the student's arrival. The more complete the information is, the greater the chance is for the student to have a successful experience. For let-ters and forms that can be sent to the cooperating teacher, see Appendix C, page 109ff.

Having a cooperating teacher decline to meet with you may be difficult for you to handle. You may find the thought of any confron-tation hard to accept. Perhaps it is the cooperating teacher who feels a sense of insecurity in your presence. She may be new to her job. She may feel that she doesn't want you to observe her while you are observing your student. Perhaps the cooperating teacher has felt threatened just by your presence.

Recently I had a student at a small center in rural New York. There were only six children in the class. The room was large and totally disorganized. There were no visible play centers. There were no easels, no sand or water table, no library shelf where books were displayed with their jackets facing out. The small amount of blocks had no accessories. There was very little of interest for the children to do. The children were running wild. My student was a sensitive and soft-spoken woman. The cooperating teacher, Ana, was scattered and seemed short on patience with the children.

On my second visit, I was delighted. I congratulated the two of them on all the changes that they had made after the initial conference. They had set up a library, a block area, and a pretend area. Some pieces, a small sink and cabinet, had been refurbished. They had replaced broken or missing knobs. Best of all, the children were involved in their work. The teacher/director spoke with me while we were out on the playground. He had been inspired by what had gone on in Ana's room. He was going to tackle his own room that very week. Everyone was excited. I was elated. I thought to myself: "I have really helped these teachers make their rooms better places for children." Then something happened. When I arrived at my third and final visit, my student was the only other adult in the room. Was Ana sick? No. Did she ever come into the room while I was there? No. Was she in the building? Yes. What had gone wrong? Did I come on too strong? Did I move too fast? I will never be quite sure. But there's one thing I do know: what you see and hear may not always be the *full* picture.

Working with a Resistant Director

Within any group of centers there will be directors who are open, cooperative, and delighted to have you present. And in this same group there will be directors who will make themselves scarce when you are around. Just as the cooperating teacher has the choice to work with you or not, the director has that same option. When you introduce yourself on your first site visit, you can speak of your willingness to exchange ideas. This leaves the next move up to him. Either

Mentoring Early Childhood Educators

the opportunity will materialize or it won't. The resistant director will simply not offer the invitation. Here again, this decision must be treated with the greatest respect. This is *his* center. This is *his* choice.

Accommodating Different Learning Styles

Because people learn in different ways, it behooves the supervisor to try to gain information from each student about her own method of comprehension. To make sure that you have current knowledge, you may want to review each student's essay titled, "What I Want You to Know About Me." In this way you can immediately become aware if learning problems exist, if the student is seeking remedial help or is presently receiving it. It is also an opportunity for Kiri to share with you thoughts about herself, her family, and her passion in life. A student often welcomes this opportunity to share personal information with a supervisor. However, on the off chance that someone takes this as an invasion of privacy, you can let the student know that the assignment is not mandatory. A student can also substitute an oral discussion instead of the paper, if that is more to her liking. With this knowledge about different learning styles, you can make accommodations. You can suggest many hands-on projects if a student learns best by doing. Very often, working alongside fellow students, sharing and discussing ideas in small groups, can lead to a greater understanding of the subject. If, through the papers she writes, *you* determine that a student needs extra help, you can direct her to the appropriate person within the college.

Serious Questions for the Supervisor

There may be a *rare* occasion when you ask yourself, "Do I see my student as a committed professional? Has she, in my opinion, chosen the right field of endeavor? Will she be a positive influence and role model for young children?" Almost always the answer is yes. However, if the answer is no, then there is a difficult but necessary task ahead . . . to think about the *possibility* of counseling the student out of the program. This is a complicated process, one that varies with each institution of learning. (1) *Make sure* that you are following the protocol that has been established where you teach. (2) Also be aware of all the *legal ramifications* that such a move may bring into play. This is serious business. For each student, there should be a paper trail of her work. (3) Determine if a student performance report has been filed. This form can be filled out at any time during the semester. There are also mid-term and end-of-term evaluation forms that the cooperating teacher fills out. (See Appendix C, page 109, for samples of all three forms.)

In the chain of events that follows, the first order of business could be that the cooperating teacher speaks to the student to alert the student of her concerns about her work. Then the cooperating teacher could call the college and speak with the chair of early childhood curriculum or the curriculum chair field placement coordinator. Next the early childhood curriculum chair would contact the course work professor and the field supervisor. Once everyone has been alerted to the problem, the student will meet with the chair of early childhood curriculum and one other member of the faculty who is closely involved with the student. Throughout all discussions, documentation of the student's performance will be scrutinized. Counselors may also be called in to work with the student on an individual basis. This is difficult and unsettling work. Fortunately, it is a rare occurrence. This process is often avoided because it is highly time-consuming and complex and it could have repercussions that could affect faculty members of the college. Because you care deeply about your student and her future, you will make every effort, along with Kiri, to think about her strengths. You will want to try to help her think of how she could use her abilities in an allied or different field. Your support can play an integral and meaningful role for her.

Caring for Students While Caring for Yourself

Because you are a people person, and because you are in a helping profession, your natural inclination is to give a great deal of yourself.

You teach because you are compelled to. You want to inspire all of your students to work with children. However, because you are a dedicated and caring individual, you may create a problem for yourself. Can you be too empathetic? Do you need to think about ways to guard against becoming too emotionally involved with your student? One of the things that you must be careful about is bringing your student's problems home with you. As with many things, this is a discipline, but one that needs your consideration. What can happen if you become too deeply involved in Kiri's life? Will you seek excuses for her, even though you know she is not fulfilling her obligation to the college? Will you let her slide through with a D when you know she should fail the course? Will you shy away from making that difficult decision because you know some of the possible consequences that decision could bring? Perhaps a way for you to protect yourself is to constantly remind yourself why you entered this profession and to recall the *responsibilities* that you assumed. It is part of your position and professionalism to ensure that *only* the most qualified people are launched into this field to educate our children.

Helping the Student Leave Her Placement

A more common issue that you will confront is helping the student leave her classroom and the children who have been so endearing to her. Just as a teacher helps a young child leave a supportive center and her beloved teachers, so must you help your student move on. Very often the cooperating teacher and the children plan a surprise celebration, to mark the student teacher's last day in class. Often the children make drawings with messages that the cooperating teacher compiles into a book for a parting gift. Perhaps they will make cupcakes, corn bread, or carrot cake, whatever is the student's favorite confection. It will be a good-bye party. Now, what can the student do in return to make her leave-taking easier, to give back something of herself? What can she do for the children, in a tangible way, so that they will remember her? Perhaps the most important thing to think about *first* is talking with them in advance of the final day. She can let the children know how hard it is for her to say good-bye, and how much being in class with them has meant to her. Kiri can also tell them what her plans are for the summer and how she is looking forward to them. She can give each child a card with her name, address, phone number, and a pretty sticker so they can stay in touch. If she would like, she could also write a story for them of all the memories she will carry away with her. She, too, could do some cooking and bring in a treat to share with the children. She could purchase a book or game or something she wants to add to the pretend area. She could use her vivid imagination to let the children know how special her time with them has been. Leave-takings are important events to acknowledge, as life is a series of separations. Let Kiri know that, although saying good-bye will be difficult, she can begin to joyfully anticipate what is coming next, just as she wants the children to do as they move on.

More Challenges as Opportunities

You may have been in classrooms that were disorganized and drab, where curriculum was nonexistent, and where the children were running wild. In such cases, the cooperating teacher may be overwhelmed and may be neither asking for nor receiving support from her director. The question here is where to begin, as there is so much that calls for attention and change. Room arrangement may be a good place to start. Then, both teachers and children can visually recognize that organization and meaning have been introduced into their world. What follows will come more gradually—introducing ideas and props that will interest children, involve them in play, and develop into a curriculum. The pivotal question you must consider is whether or not you feel comfortable in your role as a supervisor to offer direction to the cooperating teacher.

You may encounter centers without easels, where art materials are not accessible, where cooking projects are unheard of, and where woodworking is considered too dangerous. There are rooms where children stand in line, waiting and waiting. Boys are on one side, girls on another, and they are not allowed to talk among themselves. There are rooms where children eat sugary snacks and then put their

Mentoring Early Childhood Educators

hands on top of their heads to signify that they are finished. There are classrooms where children are seated at tables and given points and treats for completing their work first. In those same classrooms, the children who need more time to finish assignments are clustered together, and neither praise nor commendation comes to them.

You will visit centers that hold educational views that are substantially different from yours. Their goals for the children do not include a freedom of expression in their work or in their words. Their emphasis is on practicing listening skills, following directions, and completing assigned tasks. They have rooms that are filled with activity done in an orderly fashion. They have relatively silent rooms where children are often reminded to talk in well-modulated voices. There is no excitement or display of emotion there. There will be times to just appreciate the good points that you find: The beauty of the room that is well designed and tastefully decorated with fabrics in muted colors. The well-conceived and well-executed wooden manipulatives. The wealth of factual knowledge that the children have absorbed. There are times to leave well enough alone, to acknowledge that it takes all kinds of schools to accommodate the various philosophies that parents have.

The more difficult challenge is when you witness a lack of respect for a child, when a child is ridiculed in front of his peers. You may see a cooperating teacher throw up her hands in despair, look right at you, and say: "I just don't know what to do with Ramon." Situations like this call for your best judgment. Will you accept the challenge?

A portion of any job is dealing with the challenging issues. It is important to see the challenges as opportunities and figure out how to go about implementing change. It's also important to know when to back off, to accept that you will not be able to make a difference—and to concentrate your efforts elsewhere.

Summary

Some of the challenging issues that the supervisor faces include working with a resistant student, cooperating teacher, or director. You will also, in discovering the different learning styles that your student teachers have, need to make accommodations for them. You will, on a *rare* occasion, need to think about the possibility of counseling a student out of the program. In the event that this happens, you must proceed with utmost caution and concern, making sure that you follow established guidelines set by the college where you work. You must also make sure that you fully understand the legal ramifications of such an action. You will talk with your student about leaving her field placement site. Finally, you will want to think about all the various challenges you encounter as opportunities to implement change—a time to bring positive forces into play that will benefit both adults and children.

Reflective Questions

1. Are there additional questions that you feel should be asked of the student in order to learn more about her resistance?

2. What would you include if you formulated two more questions for the midterm or final evaluation form?

3. Do you think that you should be more aggressive in your approach to the director? How?

4. You have just learned that one of your students has extreme difficulty in taking tests. What alternatives might you suggest to the course work professor to accommodate this student?

5. What else could you suggest that could be done to help the student who is having serious problems at her field placement site?

6. If you have had trouble in the past with becoming too close to a student, what new strategies will you use to retain your professionalism?

7. What do you find is the most difficult area of your work? How will you go about making it less stressful?

8. What are your areas of resistance, and what can you do to change them?

 *Finding a Balance*

Objectives

After reading this chapter, you should understand

- the importance of putting forth your best effort;
- that spending extended periods of time in the classroom directly correlates with the effectiveness of the supervision process;
- that there are several ways to reinforce your commitment;
- that there are strategies that can help you reach your goals;
- that successes yield great satisfactions as well as spur you on; and
- that maintaining a delicate balance with all the key players is a vital component in your work.

Working with adults is very similar in many ways to working with young children. All human beings have the need to be respected and listened to. All human beings need to be talked to and nurtured with ideas and compassion. Most people respond positively to another person's interest in their work, their accomplishments, their dreams.

As your student's supervisor, you have shared a semester to-gether. You have helped your student from those first tentative days of uncertainty to become a more surefooted and confident teacher.

Your student has shared his goals and concerns with you. You have shared your goals and concerns with him. You have worked together to create a better learning climate for the children in the classroom. You have worked together to create a sense of harmony between your student and the lead teacher within the classroom. You have encouraged the use of new ideas or innovative ways to gain a different perspective. You have talked about how difficult it is to implement change and that some routines will always remain the same. You have read your student's journal writing, so you understand the depth and breadth of his feelings about his daily work. You know what obstacles he has confronted during the semester. You have gained an in-depth perspective about your student's personal and professional growth. You have certainly come to respect one another for who you are as individuals.

In addition to all the responsibilities that the supervisor feels for her student, there is, as originally stated, an obligation of the college that the student attends. Each individual should be placed in a classroom where the cooperating teacher models the kind of teaching that is respectful of all children's needs and abilities. If possible, the cooperating teacher should be a master teacher. Of course, there will be centers or schools where this expectation is not met. What can a supervisor do?

Going the Extra Mile

Each supervisor, believing that her student deserves the opportunity to be part of a positive learning environment, should evaluate the program where her student has been placed. By doing this, if there are classrooms that do not model appropriate learning practices, she can recommend they be eliminated from the list of approved placement sites. All this information should be shared with the chair of the early childhood curriculum program, the field placement coordinator, and whoever else has input regarding where the student is placed. For the benefit of the college program, each supervisor could also be requested to visit two or three new classrooms, with a view toward expanding and/or upgrading the present list of placement sites. In this way the supervisor would have greater input into the professional life of her student. A checklist for a site evaluation follows:

Site Evaluation Checklist

An environment in which:

- [ ] Safety and cleanliness are primary
- [ ] The teachers are interacting with the children in a positive way
- [ ] Children can work individually or in small groups
- [ ] The room is well organized into activity centers
- [ ] Many materials are labeled and accessible for the children
- [ ] The curriculum includes art, music and movement, block building, dramatic play, language arts, and scientific exploration
- [ ] There are both active and quiet times within the program
- [ ] The children spend an appropriate time outdoors
- [ ] Cooperation among the children is promoted
- [ ] Problem solving is highly regarded
- [ ] The children and teachers work together as a community
- [ ] Parent relations and involvement are fostered
- [ ] There is a collaborative staff
- [ ] There are professional development activities for the staff
- [ ] There is a deep respect for children and their families.

Time Well Spent

Much of your time, thought, and energy is spent in getting to know each of your students. By doing this, you can move each student along in his quest for greater understanding and skill in his chosen field. From your perspective, the best use of your time may be spent in sharing the classroom experience along with the student before the conference time. If you can, over the semester, try to spend three hour-long sessions with each student. In this way you have lived through many situations together and have a commonality of experiences from which to draw and learn. In the beginning, it will be important to make it clear that your hope is that part of your time will be spent with both the student and the cooperating teacher. Your expectation is that the three of you will work together as a team. Hopefully, you will all have the opportunity to talk through whatever situations are brought before the table.

Commitment

Your availability, by being in the classroom for extended periods of time, or by being willing to be reached by telephone, fax, email, or cell phone, helps establish your credibility and the level of your commitment. During visits to the classroom, you might be reminded of articles or books that could be helpful in the running of the class. Mailing copies to either party, instead of waiting to bring the material to the next visit, serves to underline your belief in the importance of the work that is being carried out at the center.

Strategies

There are strategies that you have used in the past which have met with great success—but not always. In most cases you would continue to strive to share information with the cooperating teacher. You may also, on a rare occasion, step in and ask if you could be of help when you see a cooperating teacher who is overwhelmed with a difficult mix of children. When you are willing to be more than just an observer, it can influence a cooperating teacher's willingness to look at different classroom strategies. In addition, when you feel it would be well received and helpful, you may ask your student to share with the cooperating teacher some of the written material from his course work at the university. These tactics can help make new inroads by offering new perspectives. There are no guarantees; there is no magic; but you ardently feel that using these different strategies is always worth a try.

Acknowledging Success

Aside from the challenges inherent within the job, there are also many successes that more than balance out the harder issues. Certainly you have inspired your student to take his job more seriously, to look in greater depth at the importance of his work. Undoubtedly, you have expanded his horizon. You have been instrumental in urging your student to complete his associate degree, finish his undergraduate work, or go on to a master's program. You have taken real pleasure in writing a recommendation for an undergraduate school, a graduate school, or a job placement. You have taken pride in being there for your student whenever he has needed you. You may even have had the ultimate satisfaction of seeing one of your outstanding students become a member of your college faculty.

You have been a student advocate. You have talked to cooperating teachers about giving your students more and more responsibility as the term progressed. You have asked that students move from handling small-group management into assuming the primary responsibility of the group. You have also requested that students be allowed to sit in on parent conferences and staff meetings to see how both are planned and executed. You have seen these requests granted. You will have worked with cooperating teachers to promote opportunities for your students to work with the children's family members. You have worked so that the students would be allowed more open communication with the parents, provided that the students first sought permission from the cooperating teacher. You have shared the importance of making parents feel welcome at a school. You have helped to impart the knowledge that parents need to be available as a youngster starts out in a child care program, to ease the child's transition from home to school. You have asked that students work on setting up field trips, making phone arrangements with the parents. You have wanted your students to become keenly aware of what a vital part parents play in advocating for their children's well-being. You have also helped your students become aware of the fine line of professionalism that must be drawn and maintained in order to avoid becoming too emotionally involved with the children's lives.

There have been, or will be, times when your student is already in the position of being the lead teacher. This can be a dramatically different experience. Because you are dealing directly with the person in charge, rather than an assistant or teacher-in-training, the possibility that change can occur is greatly enhanced. In these situations the teacher has been part of all previous college classroom discussions, so he is philosophically in tune with the thinking that is set forth by your college or university. The background work has already taken place.

Over the years you may have become acquainted with a number of lead teachers and directors so that bonds of mutual trust and admiration have already been established. You greet each other as old friends. Your talks with directors can often be the most productive of all. Here you have the possibility that your ideas will be instituted in more than one classroom or throughout a child care center. Often you will find that directors are so preoccupied with decision making and administrative details that they do not have the time to sit and observe in the classroom. Because you are doing just that, you can fill a need that can prove enormously useful to them. Your openness and honesty can also help them bring into sharper focus issues that need to be clarified or rectified.

You have found that one of the greatest resources you have available is the advice of your colleagues. With your colleagues you can brainstorm issues that concern you, listen to different points of view, and come to your own determination. As colleagues you share the latest book in the field, or an old article that is still as relevant as it was the day it was written. Mainly, you share your current thinking, which is the result of your years of experience. You will also have departmental meetings, which afford you the opportunity to gather as a group and exchange ideas. In many ways it is comforting to know that *you* have a support system too!

Summary

It is at many different levels that you put your expertise to work with the student, the cooperating teacher, the director, and your colleagues. You strive to open up the lines of communication and have many people communicate with you. You want to question why things happen in a certain way or don't happen—and have many questions asked of you. You observe, write about, and discuss what you have seen and felt, and you want others to observe, write about, and discuss with you what they have seen and felt. You want to do all that you are empowered to do to create a community of learners, to make a classroom better for children, always remembering that part of this work is to maintain the highest standards as you diligently mentor your students and teachers-in-training.

Reflective Questions

1. What other topics would you address that could help you do a better job?

2. What are some other ways that you have found successful for reinforcing your commitment? Describe.

3. If you would be willing to sit down with your colleagues to discuss strategies for a successful supervision, how and when will you set this up?

4. Now that you have read this collaborative model of supervision, what will you do differently when you work with a student?

5. What will you do for yourself to gain or maintain a good balance between your professional commitment and your personal life?

6. Would you consider writing to me so that we could have a dialogue to improve the mentoring or supervision process? Where do we think alike? Where do we differ?

Epilogue

It is my fond hope that *Mentoring Early Childhood Educators: A Handbook for Supervisors, Administrators, and Teachers* will offer an avenue for those in early childhood education to open up dialogues with one another. It is also my wish to be part of those dialogues. This can be accomplished by either contacting me by email at carolbhillman67@yahoo.com or expressing your thoughts to Heinemann. I feel that we have much to learn from one another. May the journey continue.

Appendix A

Sample Observations

Sample Observation 1

Louise and Carolyn,

Thank you for welcoming me to the Early Childhood Center at Leverett. What a long-awaited pleasure.

Let me share with you some of my reactions to the visit. First of all, the building itself is so homey, so well situated, it bespeaks a certain comfort level, despite the cut-up space in the former kitchen. As I entered the door I heard the chatter of parakeets, which set such a joyful tone right from the very start.

I am always taken with the warmth of wood and how important it is in creating a caring environment. Wooden floors and wooden accessories mellow over time, inherently giving off a message that "If you care for me, I'll be around for a long time." Do you know how unusual it is just to see wooden chairs? I also appreciate a round table, like the one in your front room. It is somehow "softer" with its curves and more welcoming than the conventional rectangular ones.

There are so many things in the room that drew my eyes toward them: the hornet's nest and magnifying glass, the papier-mâché tree in the corner, the framed artwork of a child, the self-portraits in the hallway, the wooden block accessories, along with the book *I Read Signs*, the ant farm, the new light box, and so on. Putting all the above together, along with other things that I will discuss, says one thing very clearly: We are in the presence of a master teacher. There is a certain tone that is set within the room, a pervasive calm that fills the air. The children are involved with one another, working and chatting at the same time, but very directed in their tasks. There is a genuine spirit of cooperation and a sense that these children are a community of learners. The tone of the room is enhanced in many ways; it has to do with how the teacher moves, her body language, her voice, and the words that are said, or left unsaid. It also has to do with expectation—what the children are doing on their own, how they are interacting with one another, and how they are being treated by the adults in the room.

For example, the children take attendance by putting their own names onto an attendance chart. The children mark where they have left off reading with their own handmade book markers. Just a word or two about group time, which is such a cornerstone of the program. Singing is such a powerful way of reinforcing the camaraderie of a group, and particularly after not having seen each other for an extended period of time. The talk about the change of seasons and what the new expectations are. The talk about consideration of others and the flowering bulbs. The discussion to incorporate Joan's idea about *stop* and *go* signs for the bathroom all add up to being respectful of people, their physical and psychological well-being, and the changing world we live in. It's all there!

Louise, I know through your words that you feel fortunate to be in this placement. You sat down with a small group of children at the art table, working along with them, holding Charlotte's paper jaguar for her. That was such a good way to have placed yourself, as you could see all the children in the room. It was good that you sat on the floor to play checkers and used the game to reinforce counting skills. You entered into a portion of dramatic play, asking about the jaguar's surgery. You also praised Talbert for his beautiful design with parquetry block, with a specific reference to the colors he used. I was wondering about Thomas; he seemed like such a solitary soul. I noticed that he had his head down on the floor at group time. What concerned me most was that I did not hear his voice.

Louise, Carolyn and I spoke briefly out on the playground about your final project. I feel sure that by the time you receive this, the two of you will have spoken about the possibility of focusing your project on a trip to the kitchen and all the related food items that you could use.

I thought the children came up with some great ideas for the pretend area. Will you follow through with some of these ideas, or will you use the pretend area to be part of the upcoming project—or do both?

So . . . once again let me say it was both refreshing and inspiring to be part of the calm but stimulating environment that has been created within your space. I look forward to our next meeting, which has been tentatively set for around noon on Thursday, November 7. Louise, please confirm this for me.

Many thanks,
Carol

March 20   Visit #2

John and Natalie,

I am really sorry that I was not at your class at 9:00 A.M. to be part of the morning group time. (On my last visit, the group time was held at 9:15 A.M.) I will make every effort to be there at 9:00 A.M. sharp on my next visit. My apologies.

I think it was a hard morning. I will try to offer you some ideas to think about and see whether you feel they are valid enough to act upon. Throughout all that follows, please be aware that I feel the two of you have unusually good communication skills and a firm foundation of working together. You have the ability it takes to move forward.

John, you read the story *If You Give a Pig a Pancake* with great enthusiasm. There was heightened interest in the story because of your interaction with the children. There were lots of questions and answers, but not too many to lose the thread of the story. You all looked really comfortable and content.

In the few minutes that we had together, we touched on snack procedures. There are so many details worth looking at. I am interested to know why each chair has a child's name on it. Are the chairs set at the table so that each child sits next to two particular children? I watched Elaine moving chairs around to her own satisfaction. My feeling is that children should do as much decision making on their own as they can age-appropriately handle. Could you allow children to sit next to a good friend if they desire, as long as it works? Obviously, if it isn't working, then it's up to the adults in the classroom to make a change for that day. John, if you are reading the story, then, Natalie, could you be setting up the snack for the children? Snack time should be a very relaxed, friendly time for conversation and exchange of ideas, as well as the pleasure of eating. A key ingredient would be to have each of you sit at a table with the children.

At one point, four men were at the back door, discussing renovations for the room. I don't know if they had been there before or not, but somehow I felt their presence should be acknowledged. This could lead to an exploration of the different jobs that people do. The children could talk about what their mommies and daddies do for their work. (I promise you this will be amusing.) Maybe you could invite one of the men into the room to talk with the children about his work. This could provide some meaty curriculum ideas. This is an opportunity for the two of you to discuss emergent curriculum. At any rate, I think something could have been said about who they were and what they were doing. That was a teachable moment.

I want to start with an overview about art projects and what they can mean in young children's lives. The years of early childhood are so significant. All three of us must agree on that vital point; otherwise we wouldn't have chosen this as our profession. I feel they are very precious years, and a time when children are allowed to be their most creative—to express their individual ideas, to show who they really are. As children grow older they are required to conform more and more to peer pressure and adult expectations. They can feel less free to express themselves. So . . . it behooves us to make the most of these early years, so that children can feel confident about doing what they want to do, artistically speaking.

When children are given a precut form, be it shamrock, heart, flower, or butterfly, it is saying to a child: "This is, for example, what a flower should look like." It is also saying, in so many words: "I can do this better than you can." I know, having seen you two in action, that there is no way in the world that you would want to convey this to the children in your class. I know you are both caring and committed people. I also know that you wanted to give the children a new experience by working with cornstarch. Now comes the challenge. How could you fulfill the goal you had in mind for the children in a different way, giving them the opportunity to experience a new medium but in a more creative way?

It was good that the art table was covered with paper, and that each shamrock was handled carefully and set out to dry. Could the children wear smocks when they are working with paint? Could there be two tables, instead of one, used as art tables, since the interest was so high?

I am concerned about Douglas. He looks so terribly pale. He also seems very angry. At one point he had a plastic basket over his face. He reminded me of a caged animal. He was kicking the plastic trains with a vengeance. Later on, he ran to the other side of the room divider, where another group was located. He was told to "go back" in a very harsh voice. I worry about what kind of message this sends to children about next-door neighbors. I wonder what the center's policy is about having children visit back and forth, and how flexible the teachers are to accommodate the different needs of children. This could be a hot topic for a staff meeting.

I have thrown out a lot of ideas to you. I hope that you will discuss them among yourselves and respond to me. I was delighted to hear that you are relabeling the manipulatives! I am enclosing a catalog, hoping that the pictures could be useful to you for future labeling. Please remember, I have great faith in your abilities.

I am looking forward to seeing you both again on Wednesday, April 17 at 9:00 A.M. for sure!

Carol

Appendix B

Sample Journal Responses

A Student's Response to Journal Seven

Journal Seven: What do you notice when children are involved in dramatic play (in the dramatic play area, outdoors, and so on)? What do they talk about? What ideas come up for them?

The dramatic play area offers children many choices in which to pretend and re-create some of their life experiences. In my field placement we always have a dramatic play area that offers general housekeeping, dress-up clothes, and writing materials. This has been the most popular place of play for both the boys and the girls.

One of our topics has been the human body. From this theme emerged forms of dramatic play such as hospital and doctors. To enhance play in this regard, we have added the following props: a skeleton, real X rays, stethoscope, thermometers, white lab jackets, pens, and prescription pads. You can often hear the language of the situation at play, such as: "The doctor is very busy, you must have a seat and wait your turn," or "Could someone take the sick person to X rays—use a wheelchair," or "I saw them do that on TV." Everyone seems to be enjoying this role acting, whether they are doctors, nurses, or sick people.

From the same human-body theme, the topic of nutrition and eating different foods has emerged. To our prop box we added the following selections: a variety of pretend fruits and vegetables for healthy choices, as well as multicultural items with which the children are already familiar. These include pizza, egg rolls, tacos, and sushi. We have also included additional telephones, cooking utensils, writing materials, cash registers, and menus. From this topic we see the world of chefs, waiters/waitresses, and guests dining in a restaurant.

Adding additional items to the dramatic area lets the children's interest develop in a creative and imaginative way.

A Student's Response to Journal Nine

Journal Nine:

1. What materials are provided and how are children using them?
2. How do you respond to children's work? What do you say? What do you think the children are learning from your reaction to their work?

Here at the West River Preschool classroom there is no clearly defined "art area." There are two easels with paper storage underneath and a nearby storage case with shelves and drawers which have crayons, markers, paper, water paint, glue, scissors, and so on. Classroom tables which are used for art are also used for lunch and snack.

Paper, crayons, and markers are always accessible and available, as are easels, but other art materials are not. How the easels are used on any given day is teacher determined. For example, whether chalk, water paint or tempera paint, or sponge-tip paint markers are put out. Children, therefore, cannot choose to use water paint if the paint markers are placed out at the easel.

Collage materials are also not accessible for the children to choose, but again rather by teacher decision based on table space available.

Play dough is made, on average once a week, in a single color; however, modeling clay has never been introduced to this classroom of children.

There are many things that I would like to change in the area of art at this center, but realistically, there just is not enough space to implement what I believe children should have access to. For example, I would like a defined "art area" with lots of table space, where finger paint, collage materials, water paint, and play dough were also accessible to children and available to use whenever they wish. I would like to see tempera paints, paint markers, watercolors, sponges, and a variety of brushes displayed near the easels for children to select from, and let the choice of media come from them. Here again, space limits us from being able to do this. To compensate, we try to offer a variety of materials on a rotational basis in order to give children access to a variety of media, but the selection of the day or week is still teacher decided.

Recently, I have started what I call a "junk art table." Here, in addition to glue, tape, scissors, and markers, a diverse assortment of items is put out (always changing and can include macaroni, buttons, bottle caps, tissue rolls, beads, small boxes or containers, felt pieces, foil . . . basically, whatever teachers bring in, and the children "create"). They are free to make whatever they wish and as many things as they desire. Of course, the center time is still predetermined; however, the child can continue on his creation the next day if he does not finish before cleanup. This has been a very successful addition to the classroom and is frequently chosen by children who previously did not often choose to do art, as well as by those who often choose other art media. It has taken some time for the children to move away from the "flat" surface creations, and some are now just starting to construct dimensional pieces and are beginning to use a wider variety of textures and colors. In a perfect world, I would have this table open daily, but again, it too is available on a rotating basis.

The response to children's artwork in this class varies from teacher to teacher. Although no comments are ever negative or down-putting. Occasionally questions are asked that are not open-ended, such as: "What is it?"or "What did you make?" I try very hard not to use these types of questions because it puts the child on the spot for an answer. What if the child didn't make a specific "thing" or has not given it a name? I rather try to engage the child in conversation about the creation by saying: "Tell me about what you made" or "I see you used . . . in your project." Asking the child: "Have you given it a name yet?" is better than "What is it called?" The first question is open and gives the child the opportunity to name it or not— no wrong answer is possible. The second question, however, requires an answer that the child may not have.

I also try to comment on the materials used or the arrangement of the materials, which shows the child that I am looking at what he did, and that what he did was important to me. This gives their creation value and fosters their self-esteem. Simply saying that the artwork is "great" or "beautiful" or "nice" gives no value to what the child created, and I always try to steer away from empty phrases.

I believe that the comments that I use regarding their expressive creations are very important to building their self-esteem and self-worth. It is not enough to just say: "You did a great job," but rather to convey the message that "You are a great person, whose individuality is respected and valued." I hope, from my comments, that they are learning to appreciate their own individuality as well as learning to respect the same in others.

Supervisor's Response at Time of Site Visit

Jennifer, you've expressed your ideas about children's artwork (really, any work!)—and your response to it—so very clearly.

I would add another thought to those you have articulated: As you indicate, the quality of our response to children's work is important. There is another level of self-esteem that comes to a child through his *own* satisfaction.

For example, it is easy to see this on the playground when a child has not been able to master a skill such as climbing to the top of a play gym. Then, one day, he *does* find himself at the top and realizes his accomplishment without anyone saying a word.

When a child completes a ten-piece puzzle for the first time, he has the direct appreciation of his growth. Last week he couldn't do that puzzle and now he is a "ten-piece expert." Block work, manipulatives, being able now to sing "that whole song" are all possible sources of that same self-esteem. Esteem without the words of the teacher. All this, inherent in a rich environment, is our responsibility.

The immediacy of this kind of accomplishment is so valuable and so honest to all of us. We sense it *ourselves* and experience the joy of our growing abilities.

Jo

A Supervisor's Response Written After the Site Visit

Owen, in reading your journal response, I am struck with several things: That the pretend area is used a great deal by both boys and girls, that there are many different themes presented to the group.

This leads me to believe that there has been a great deal of thought given to what props should be introduced in order to enhance the quality of play. Bravo!

Would you and the cooperating teacher consider taking the group on trips that would introduce the themes in a very real and exciting way? Would you consider a trip to the local hospital? The children could visit the cafeteria, the physical therapy room, the beauty parlor, and the pediatric floor with its playroom. If the timing is right, they could go inside an ambulance and see all the equipment with which the paramedics work. Then, they could end up at the nursery to see the brand-new babies. This kind of experience is a learning experience on many levels. Having had the experience of touring a hospital, it will not be so frightening if and when they ever have to have a hospital stay.

When I was a classroom teacher we took two hospital trips. We started out at a veterinary hospital, which was right across the street from the school. We always took our class guinea pig so that she could have her toenails clipped! It was a preliminary for the White Plains Hospital trip, which came later in the year. At the end of the trip our guide gave us several face masks, surgical caps, and gauze for pretending to make a cast for a broken arm or leg. All of this went right into the pretend area. The play that ensued became so much more meaningful because of the experience that the children had just had.

In the same way, if the theme of food or nutrition is being studied, would you and the cooperating teacher consider going to the supermarket, a bakery, or a small shop that makes pasta? Can you imagine the excitement and interest if you went to the local pizzeria and ordered several large pizzas to divide among the group? Then, come back to your center, and all of you together can think and talk about what you would need to set up Pete's Pizza Parlor right in your own room. That way children become truly invested in their work, because they have lived it—and they will be able to relive and expand upon it in countless ways.

Carol

Appendix C

Communications with the Cooperating Teacher

A LETTER TO THE COOPERATING TEACHER

Fall

Dear Colleague:

This letter will introduce you to our early childhood student and the process for field placement. Please review the FIELD SUMMARY SHEET together during your orientation meeting. If you consider this to be a good match and agree on a satisfactory schedule, please sign the CONTRACT. The student will return it to us and begin working as early as September 10 and no later than September 17. The student will complete **126 hours** for the semester, with **9 hours per week.** In addition, the student will notify you regarding absence and late arrival. *Missed time must be made up by the student and will be scheduled with the supervisor's agreement.*

Enclosed are the following:

- a field placement contract;

- an academic calendar;

- a field summary sheet;

- a course outline;

- a student performance report;

- a midterm evaluation; and

- a final evaluation.

Please contact us if you need information or have any questions at 555/785-6600.

Thank you for your continued cooperation and for your willingness to give our students an opportunity for learning and enrichment.

Sincerely yours,
John Drake

Your signatures confirm that you have reread, understand, and agree to the attached terms of this contract and have corrected any incorrect agency data printed above. CHANGE SITE ADDRESS IF DIFFERENT.

FIELD PLACEMENT CONTRACT

Name:_____ Soc. Sec.:_____Major:_____

Address:_____ Phone:_____

COURSES

Academic:_____

Field:_____

AGENCY

Agency Liaison:_____ Phone:_____

    Class Instructor:_____

    Faculty Liaison:_____

    Field Supervisor:_____

REMARKS

_____

_____

WORK SCHEDULE (to be filled in by agency liaison)

Days: _____ Start Date: _____

Hours: _____

Assigned Direct Supervisor (please print): _____

Signature of Assigned Supervisor: _____

Signature of Student: _____

Your signatures confirm that you have reread, understand, and agree to the attached terms of this contract and have corrected any incorrect agency data printed above. CHANGE SITE ADDRESS IF DIFFERENT.

FIELD SUMMARY SHEET

Early Childhood Curriculum

Field experience will provide students with an opportunity to:

- Develop an understanding of children as meaning makers and authors of their own learning.
- Use written observations of individual and small groups of children to explore possibilities for project work.
- Assess children's prior knowledge in order to uncover understandings and misunderstandings.
- Document children's ideas and collect samples of their work in order to understand the range of their ideas.
- Explore how the disciplines of literacy, social studies, math, art, science, and music are an integral part of project work.
- Identify room arrangements that invite and encourage a sense of wonder, exploration, and problem solving. Specifically, look at block area, library, dramatic play area, sand and water tables, and the art area.

Students are expected to:

- Maintain a journal that will include thoughts about their project work.
- Meet weekly with the cooperating teacher and share journal reflections.
- Participate in team planning and staff meetings.
- Complete and document 126 hours of fieldwork.
- Submit monthly time sheets signed by the cooperating teacher.
- Return midterm evaluations.
- Notify center or school when they are unable to attend.

Cooperating teachers are expected to:

- Meet with students on a weekly basis.
- Read student journals and provide written reflections.
- Sign monthly time sheets.
- Meet with the supervisor and student during conference times.
- Contact the field placement coordinator or the course instructor with any questions or concerns.

STUDENT PERFORMANCE REPORT

Please give copies of this form to the field placement coordinator and field liaison.

Date: _____

FIELD LIAISON REPORT:

Site Visit: _____Yes _____No   Phone Contact: _____Yes _____No

Field Liaison Name: _____

Student: _____ Course:_____ Teacher:_____

Agency: _____ Supervisor:_____

Please comment on the following:

Attendance: _____

Punctuality: _____

Attitude: _____

Performance: _____

Supervision: _____

Assignment (appropriate): _____

Problems: _____

Site Evaluation: _____

(continued on following page)

(continued from previous page)

*TEACHER REPORT:

Student: _____ Course: _____ Teacher: _____

Agency: _____ Supervisor: _____

Please comment on the following. (Comment on concerns regarding field appropriateness. Please use this form to report if a student never attended or stopped attending class.)

Attendance: _____

Attitude: _____

Performance: _____

Problems: _____

_____

_____

_____

_____

Teachers need to fill this out only if concerned about a student.

MIDTERM EVALUATION
Early Childhood Education Student Field Placement

This form must be signed by both student and cooperating teacher.

Student:_____

Agency:_____

Instructor:_____

Course:_____

Semester:_____

1. Describe the student's interactions with children (e.g., shows interest and respect, uses ap-
    propriate tone of voice, speaks at eye level). Please illustrate your response. Be specific.

    _____

    _____

    _____

    _____

    _____

2. What opportunities does the student have to practice what he or she is learning in the
    course? Please give examples from your observations (e.g., project work, written descrip-
    tions of children's behavior, collecting children's work).

    _____

    _____

    _____

    _____

    _____

(continued on following page)

(continued from previous page)

3. In what ways does the student demonstrate professional and ethical behavior (e.g., conscientious, enthusiastic, takes appropriate initiative, seeks guidance when in doubt, dresses appropriately)?

_____

_____

_____

_____

_____

ADDITIONAL COMMENTS:

_____

_____

_____

_____

_____

_____   _____
Supervisor's Signature   Date

STUDENT'S RESPONSE:

_____

_____

_____

_____

_____

_____

_____   _____
Student's Signature   Date

FINAL EVALUATION
Early Childhood Education Student Field Placement

This form must be signed by both student and cooperating teacher.

Student:_____

Agency:_____

Instructor:_____

Course:_____

Semester:_____

1. Describe the student's interactions with children (e.g., shows interest and respect, uses appropriate tone of voice, speaks at eye level). Please illustrate your response. Be specific.

_____

_____

_____

_____

_____

2. What opportunities does the student have to practice what he or she is learning in the course? Please give examples from your observations (e.g., project work, written descriptions of children's behavior, collecting children's work).

_____

_____

_____

_____

(continued on following page)

(continued from previous page)

3. In what ways does the student demonstrate professional and ethical behavior (e.g., conscientious, enthusiastic, takes appropriate initiative, seeks guidance when in doubt, dresses appropriately).

_____

_____

_____

_____

_____

4. In what ways has this student grown?

_____

_____

_____

_____

_____

5. What recommendations do you have for further growth?

_____

_____

_____

_____

_____

_____

_____

_____

_____

(continued from previous page)

ADDITIONAL COMMENTS:

_____

_____

_____

_____

_____

_____

_____

_____

_____

_____   _____

Supervisor's Signature   Date

STUDENT'S RESPONSE:

_____

_____

_____

_____

_____

_____

_____

_____

_____

_____

_____

_____   _____

Student's Signature   Date

References and Suggested Readings

Cadwell, Louise B. 1997. *Bringing Reggio Emilia Home*. New York: Teachers College Press.

————. *Bringing Learning to Life*. 2003. New York: Teachers College Press.

Carson, Rachel. 1956. *The Sense of Wonder*. New York: Harper and Row.

Church, F. F. *The New York Sun*, September 21, 1897, editorial.

Cohen, Dorothy, and Virginia Stern. 1983. *Observing and Recording the Behavior of Young Children*. New York: Teachers College Press.

Cuffaro, Harriet. 1995. *Experimenting with the World*. New York: Teachers College Press.

Davis, Ursula T. 1997. *Blocks: The Cornerstone of an Early Childhood Curriculum*. New York: Childcraft.

Edelman, Marion W. 1992. *The Measure of Our Success*. Boston: Beacon.

Edwards, Carolyn, and Lella Gandini. 1998. *The Hundred Languages of Children*. Greenwich, CT: Ablex.

Ginott, Haim. 1972. *Teacher and Child*. New York: Macmillan.

Helm, Judy, and Lilian Katz. 2001. *Young Investigators: The Project Approach in the Early Years*. New York: Teachers College Press.

Himley, Margaret, and Patricia F. Carini. 2000. *From Another Angle*. New York: Teachers College Press.

Jones, Elizabeth, and Gretchen Reynolds. 1992. *The Play Is the Thing*. New York: Teachers College Press.

Koralek, Derry, Laura Corker, and Diane T. Dodge. 1993. *The What, Why and How of High Quality Early Childhood Education*. Washington, DC: National Association for the Education of Young Children.

Pignatelli, Frank, and Susanna Pflaum. 1994. *Experiencing Diversity*. Thousand Oaks, CA: Corwin.

Shaheen, JoAnn C., and Carolyn C. Spence. 2002. *Take Charge! Advocating for Your Child's Education*. Albany, NY: Delmar Thomson Learning.

Stone, Jeannette G. 2001. *Building Classroom Community*. Washington, DC: National Association for the Education of Young Children.

Trabwitz, Sidney, and Maureen P. Robins. 2003. *The Good Teacher Mentor*. New York: Teachers College Press.

Yelland, Nicola. 2000. *Promoting Meaningful Learning*. Washington, DC: National Association for the Education of Young Children.

Zachary, Lois J. 2000. *The Mentor's Guide*. San Francisco: Jossey-Bass.